The Unabridged Dictionary of Sarcastic Definition

2008-2009 Edition

The Unabridged Dictionary of Sarcastic Definition

2008-2009 Edition

David Gudgeon

iUniverse, Inc.
New York   Bloomington

iUniverse books may be ordered through booksellers or by contacting:

iUniverse
1663 Liberty Drive
Bloomington, IN 47403
www.iuniverse.com
1-800-Authors (1-800-288-4677)

ISBN: 978-1-4401-3023-6 (sc)
ISBN: 978-1-4401-3025-0 (ebook)

Printed in the United States of America

iUniverse rev. date: 03/09/2009

To all the coffee tables across America and abroad where this book will be available to occupy the stagnant minds of the house guests of the people who bought it as those guests patiently sit on the couch and wait and wait and wait for their hosts to hurry the hell up.

*What? You never could figure out the right thing to say
at the right time? Well, maybe I can help.*

<u>Special Note</u>

Be aware that this book is neither unabridged
nor is it a real dictionary.
Keep in mind that this book has been written all in good
fun and purely for entertainment, and that no harm or insult
is really intended, and that what has been written herein
may not necessarily be the author's beliefs, as some of it may
be considered insulting, and downright racy, depending
on your point of view. So, in other words, *suck it up!*

A: If you don't know this one, a dictionary won't help you.

Abacus: An antique calculator.

Abandon: What politicians do to urban renewal projects immediately upon being elected.

Abbess: The head knuckle cracker.

Abbey: Where the head knuckle cracker (abbess) lives.

Abbot: The male version of an abbess.

Abdomen: Where you get hit in the locker room.

Abdominal: The type of pain you feel after eating fast food.

Abduction: A task usually carried out by aliens.

Ability: What most of the workforce lacks.

Ablaze: What certain parts of you feel like when seated on the "throne" (depending on your diet).

Abnormal: What about 90 percent of teenagers are.

Abode: Fancy word for yo' crib.

Abominable: The armpit of the person holding the strap above your seat on the bus.

Abomination: The school lunch menu.

Abortion: Something you can't do when it's legal but can when it's not.

Above: What many clergy-people think they are when it comes to morals.

Abreast: Where the white meat is.

Absenteeism: A common occurrence among high school students.

Absolute: What the absent high school students are probably drinking.

Absorb: What is done with the "absolute."

Absorbent: The underwear of the high school student after he passes out from the "absolute."

Abstain: What the high school student is not likely to try to do with the opposite sex.

Abstinence: Good in principle but unlikely in practice.

Abstract: Art for the untalented.

Absurd: Thinking that your vote counts in an election (refer to what happened in the 2000 presidential primary and then get a book on government and study the Electoral College).

Abundance: What the wealthy seem to have in every area of life.

Abuse: What you can do with authority.

Abusive: What many husbands are before their prison careers.

Abut: The focus of many male eyes.

Abyss: Where your socks go at the Laundro-mat.

Academy: Where you send your rotten kid when he gets to be too much trouble.

Accelerate: What you do on the highway after you pass the speed trap.

Accent: What every cab driver in the country has.

Acceptable: What we pretend things that are "politically correct" are.

Access: What every company and government on earth has to your personal information, while you do not.

Accessory: What you can be to a crime, even if you didn't do it, and still end up in jail.

Accident: How you get a free check at work.

Acclaim: Something you get for writing a lousy book or acting badly in a movie.

Accommodate: What the U.S. government does by having urban professionals learn every language on earth instead of making immigrants to America learn English the same way other countries force us to learn theirs.

Accomplice: The guy you "roll" on so that you can get a reduced sentence.

Accomplishment: Something that is very difficult to achieve with our modern children expecting praise without commitment or positive results.

Accordion: An ancient festival device used by tribal nerds in leather shorts.

Accost: What the prosecutor does to the witness.

Accountable: Something most parents don't hold their children when they act up in school.

Accountant: The guy who knows where your money goes when you're not smart enough to count it yourself.

Accumulate: What the average American does with valueless modern collectibles.

Accuracy: Something that is often seriously lacking in computer operating systems' security protocols.

Accused: What the neighborhood kids are every time something happens to your flower bed.

Accuser: Usually some asshole.

Accustomed: What you get to be with regard to harsh urban living conditions when no one ever does anything about them.

Ace: The card the dealer always seems to have.

Ache: What your head does after ten hours of work.

Achievement: See Accomplishment.

Acknowledgement: Something that is very hard to get a judge to give you when you really need some sympathy in court.

Acorn: A word that is easier to understand than the next one you read.

Acotyledons: A word you would use only if you were a botanist, so don't worry about it.

Acquaintance: What most people really are, as opposed to being your actual friend.

Acquire: What you do with property when you are filthy rich.

Acquisition: A fancy word for succeeding with the word above.

Acquit: What you hope the jury does so you won't be toast.

Acre: Worth about $250,000 in the city and about $2,000 in the country.

Acrimonious: What this dictionary is.

Acrobat: Someone who is really cool when she is your girlfriend.

Acrobatic: Why you think she is cool.

Act: Something you put on when you show up drunk at your girlfriend's house at three in the morning.

Action: What your girlfriend takes against you with a frying pan for showing up drunk at three in the morning.

Activity: What there is a lot of with that frying pan your girlfriend uses when you show up drunk at three in the morning.

Actor: You had better be a damn good one if the above three definitions pertain to you.

Actress: The female version.

Acupressure: The foot rubs you will be giving your girlfriend for the next three months while you try to apologize for showing up drunk at three in the morning.

Adamant: The material of the average teenager's skull when you are trying to tell him or her something important.

Adam's apple: A good place to bust a guy when he won't leave you alone.

Adapt: What really small activist groups expect everyone else to do when they don't like how they live.

Add: What most cashiers can't do without a calculator (see the automatic change counter in your local market).

Addict: There's one in every family.

Addition: Something you get to your family when you forget your "raincoat."

Additive: It's in everything you eat.

Address: There are too many people in the world without one.

Adept: What you have to be in order to write your own dictionary (pun intended).

Adhesive: What your bandage claims to be before it falls off.

Adjunct: A term for college professors who are not on the full-time faculty list because their credentials are better than the professors who are.

Adjustment: Something we make too many of when it comes to the Constitution.

Administer: What your mom does with that nasty medicine.

Administration: A fancy word for those company executives who screw up your job.

Admirable: Someone who can write his own book (hint hint).

Admiration: Often showered on entirely the wrong people.

Admit: Something that would make life easier if people did it more often.

Adobe: Cheap building material.

Adolescent: Someone who used to be manageable before corporal punishment became a political issue.

Adopt: What you do with a foreign policy that has nothing to do with your own country.

Adoption: When you pay to get a child who no one wants from another country because they won't give you the ones that no one wants in this country.

Adrift: What you are in bullshit at work.

Adult: What most grownups don't act like.

Adultery: The act of ruining your marriage.

Advance: Something you should never try to get on your pay unless you want to look like a jerk.

Advancement: You can get this with your company one of two ways: knowing someone or blowing someone.

Advantage: You take this with the employee described above.

Adventure: You can experience this walking down the street depending on what kind of neighborhood you are living in.

Adversary: The thug that causes the adventure described above.

Advertise: How you brainwash people.

Advertisement: A test for stupidity that we often fail.

Advertiser: A person whose job it is to exploit the average TV viewer's lack of intelligence.

Advertising: One of the ways in which the end of the world will be brought about.

Advice: What you wish most of your relatives would keep to themselves.

Affair: A good way to end your marriage.

Affectionate: What you could have been to prevent the above.

Affirmative: What a smart-ass soldier says instead of "yes."

Afloat: Something that is pretty hard to stay, in today's economy.

Africa: Where most convenience store managers come from.

Afterbirth: Eeewww!.

Afternoon: The time most people wish they could set their alarm clock for.

Afterward: Usually, when you really think about what you have been doing.

Age: Works great for wine and cheese but not so good for us.

Aggravating: Your kids, your job, your taxes, your bills, your friends, your spouse, etc., etc., etc.

Agility: Something that many officials in sports lack while they sit there and judge everyone else.

Agony: Listening to your spouse's problems.

Ahoy: A really gay-sounding way of saying "hello."

Air-bladder: Sounds painful, doesn't it?

A la mode: The best way to have pie.

Alarm: Only works in your car during a thunderstorm.

Alarm clock: My arch nemesis. Should be shut off with a shotgun in the morning.

Alcohol: The devil in a bottle.

Alcoholic: Self-destructive buffoon hell bent on blaming everyone but himself for his own idiocy.

Alcoholism: They call it a disease, but I thought you caught a disease.

Algebra: How you tie your brain in a knot even though you thought you knew math.

Alibi: Something you can only afford when you are wealthy enough.

Alien: Either jumps the fence or flies over it, depending on what part of the country you are in.

Alimony: The act of being forced to pay for your mistake for years after he or she has moved out.

Allegation: Often enough for a conviction.

Allergy: A good excuse when you know how to use it.

Alligator: Florida salamander.

Allowable: What most behaviors are if you can afford it.

Allowance: Getting paid for nothing.

Alluring: Any other woman, after you have tied the knot.

Almightiness: What you see in the mirror, (when you're CEO of a *Fortune* 500 company).

Alone: People without deodorant.

Alphabetical: An order of arrangement that most public school students can't figure out.

Alternative: It used to mean a choice but now its rock music.

Amateur: Any doctor you meet when you are admitted to the emergency room.

Amazement: What you experience when the real doctor shows up after you're admitted to the emergency room.

Amazing: The circumstances if your doctor's diagnosis makes any sense to you.

Amazon: The girl who used to beat you up in third grade.

Ambition: Something the youth of this country seem to be sadly lacking.

Ambrosia: Really decent ice cream!

Ambulance: The most expensive cab ride you will ever have.

Ambush: Any interview with the press or law officers.

Amendment: Seems noble enough until you put it into practice and screw everything up.

American: Anyone in America, even though they are not from here; and the ones who *are* from here are not really Americans anyway, because they were here before it *was* America, and the ones who are not but are born here call themselves firstly by whatever country their parents came from, even though they are not that nationality since they were born here, (confused?).

Ammonia: Grandma pours it in her bath water.

Ammunition: What politicians give the press every time they open their mouths.

Amoeba: Smarter than most people who volunteer unwanted advice.

Amplifier: That thing your kid keeps in the garage that makes the neighbors call the cops at 2 a.m.

Amputation: The act of being taken to divorce court.

Amusing: Your paycheck to everyone else.

Anal: That thing your wife won't let you have no matter how much you beg.

Anarchist: The TV meteorologist, every time there is a drizzle.

Anarchy: What any daycare center is in the state of.

Anchor: You get one for every wedding band.

Ancient: Deli-style food in any convenience store.

Anesthetic: Costs so much you wish doctors still hit you on the head to put you out.

Angel: If human, a devil in disguise.

Anguish: What you feel when you open your cell-phone bill.

Animal: What your kids eat like if you are foolish enough to take them out to dinner.

Anniversary: Easily turned into hell on earth if you forget it.

Annoyance: Television advertising.

Anonymous: The guy who hits your car in the parking lot while you're shopping.

Ant: You to any bank or big corporation.

Antenna: That thing you keep breaking off of your cell phone.

Anthem: That thing with all the words your kids don't know the definitions to, (if they can even read it), but they are forced to memorize it and sing it at school.

Anti-aircraft: Taking the bus.

Antiquarian: Fancy word for old shit.

Antique: Old junk until you have it appraised.

Antiseptic: Parents pour it on little children's booboos in order to secretly torture them.

Anus: The cavity in your body that, after you crash your father's car, will become so tight it would take a freight train to pull a needle out of it.

Anvil: Your foot during the crash mentioned above.

Anxiety: What comes over you when you realize you need to tell your dad you crashed his car.

Aorta: Feels like it's going to burst when you actually tell your dad you crashed his car.

Apish: Your daughter's boyfriend.

Apologetic: What management forces retail store workers when confronted with a miserable customer's bad attitude.

Apology: What the miserable customer actually owes the store worker, while the worker is apologizing to him.

Appalling: Modern music.

Appeal: The right of a condemned man to waste court time and taxpayer money.

Appetite: Usually ruined by the salad and bread you eat while waiting for your meal in a fancy restaurant.

Applause: That thing they make the audience do on talk shows to make them seem entertaining.

Applicant: Usually someone who is wasting your time, if you work in human resources.

Application: A paper that generally asks way too much personal information.

Appointment: That thing you are always at least nine minutes late for.

Approachable: The ugly chick at the club.

Approval: What you will never get for your fiancé from your dad.

Aptitude: A test they use to determine your child's intelligence, rather than considering his knowledge or ability.

Aquarium: Fish prison.

Archeologist: The coolest job in the world after *Raiders of the Lost Ark* came out.

Arctic: Any inner city apartment in winter.

Aristocracy: Something it seems we are quickly resurrecting.

Armor: Something inner city kids should be wearing to school.

Armpit: A really unusual place for hair (don't you think?).

Arouse: Something it was hard to get Grandpa to do before Viagra.

Arrogant: A little, but I think I have it under control now.

Arrogance: Something most people display at work if you give them any kind of title, no matter how lowly it is.

Art: The hardest and most unappreciated thing to produce.

Artery: Swells when Dad gets the bills.

Artichoke: A miserable plant you eat when you think you're cultured.

Artificial: Supplementary boobs.

Artist: The poorest brilliant person you will ever meet.

Asinine: Most explanations given you by your teenager.

Ass: Where the boot goes if you make the slightest bit of a mistake on the job.

Assassin: Anyone ranking lower than you in the office.

Assessment: The excuse they use to take your job.

Assets: What you are seriously lacking when you lose that job.

Associate: What most people you call your friend really are.

Assumption: The prelude to most serious problems.

Asthma: What you got from your parents when they smoked in the house.

Astonishing: The salaries of most movie actors.

Astrology: Bullshit.

Atheism: Denial (usually undone fairly quickly if anything serious happens).

Atheist: Typically, a very angry person.

Athlete: The really fit person that all the out-of-shape people mock.

Attaché case: A fancy word for that thing you carry your lunch to work in.

Attorney: Bullshit artist.

Attractive: Something your spouse stopped being after the wedding.

Audience: Something you always seem to have if you have an argument in public.

Autobiography: Self-righteous bullshit.

Average: The actual appearance of most self-centered people.

Avoidance: A skill most people master whenever someone is trying to serve a subpoena.

Awake: The more exhausted you are, the more of this you become.

Babble: What Grandma does when she thinks no one is around.

Baby: Anywhere from newborn to about twenty-four years old, depending on how spoiled the kid is.

Bachelor: Official title for an older gay man.

Backbone: Seriously lacking in the youth of today.

Background: Something not very savory in the case of most people.

Backwoods: A frightful place to be after having seen the movie *Deliverance.*

Bacon: An extra buck if they put it on your burger.

Bad: Convenience store coffee.

Baffled: Police detectives in any case that doesn't involve someone wealthy.

Baggage: Something your spouse drags along behind him or her when entering the relationship (usually much larger than it first appears).

Bail: Often money poorly spent.

Bailout: Winning a popularity contest.

Bait: An attractive police officer on a street corner.

Baldness: A disease affecting most men that causes them to spend countless amounts of money on useless chemical products and little carpets.

Ballistic: Any co-worker after having been passed over for promotion for the third time.

Ballot: Something that starts out simple but turns out to be ridiculously complicated (and in many countries, cast by a dead relative).

Baklava: Food of the gods; I could live off of this stuff forever (one cool point to the Greeks).

Band: What your teenager is trying to form in the garage while he's keeping the neighborhood up in the middle of the night with that entire miserable no-talent racket.

Bandit: The person in charge of the division that figures APR for credit cards.

Banjo: A guitar on Ritalin.

Bank: An institution that charges you for using your own money.

Baptism: Freeing a baby from sin before he or she has any.

Bar: A place that is often more inviting than going home.

Barbarian: A child at the dinner table.

Barbecue: An event whereby Dad spends large sums of money to ruin good meat.

Bare: The best way to be spanked.

Barmaid: Someone you had best keep your hands off of if you don't want the bouncer to tie you in a knot.

Barnacles: They look like those things on Grandpa's elbows.

Baseball: America's national pastime, back before professional wrestling and monster trucks.

Basement: Where you lock up the dog when you should be walking him.

Bastard: Little brother.

Bat: A nocturnal creature whose frightening abilities are over rated.

Bath: An activity that requires the attention of more people than you would think.

Battering ram: A shopping cart to your new car.

Beach: A dumping ground for hospital waste.

Bear: What your uncle's roommate calls him, (in private).

Bearable: Something that most jobs hardly are.

Beardless: What you wish your aunt was every time she tries to kiss you at reunions.

Beautiful: Nature untouched by man.

Bed: A place most adults don't spend enough time in.

Beer: America's other national pastime.

Beggar: Any relative for whom you are not home when they call (if you're smart).

Behavior: Something that too many parents let their children run amok with in public.

Believer: What many pretend to be when in church.

Belly: Not as cute with a piercing as you have been led to believe.

Belt: A device that, if used more often, would cut down on outbursts in toy stores and the candy aisle at the supermarket.

Benevolence: An extremely rare phenomenon.

Bestiality: Really nasty form of entertainment often found on the Internet.

Bet: A waste of good resources.

Bewilderment: What a politician at a press conference shows upon being asked a real question by a reporter in the audience.

Biased: Most judges during trial.

Bible: A very exploited book.

Bigamy: Only good in Salt Lake City or the Middle East.

Bigotry: An extremely nasty hobby practiced by many self-proclaimed church-going folk.

Bilingual: Quickly becoming a requirement for elementary school teachers.

Billion: Something that would make life easier if I had one.

Biology: A really tough class they make you take in college.

Birthday: Overrated self-glorification.

Bitterness: What you feel when you find out the guy they just hired is making more than you and you've been working there for five years.

Biweekly: A really shitty way to get paid.

Blab: What your wife does on the phone for three hours a night.

Blackmail: A profession that exploits things like the photos of you at the office Christmas party.

Black market: Where your uncle gets all those electronics for cheap.

Black sheep: Me to my family.

Bladder: Always seems to be really full when there are no clean public restrooms.

Bleach: That stuff you always seem to spill on your colors at the laundry.

Bleak: Our future if we don't do something constructive about it now.

Blizzard: A good excuse not to go to work.

Bloated: Any person leaving a buffet.

Blob: Any person who frequents a buffet.

Blockhead: The neighbor kid when you have to watch him.

Blond: Someone who is hard to spot with so many fakes out there.

Bloodmoney: All money.

Blood-shot: The eyes of most teenagers on Saturday morning.

Bloodthirsty: Divorce attorneys.

Blubber: A layer of cushion commonly found on adults; it comes from eating too much crap instead of real food.

Bluff: How you get out of traffic tickets.

Boardinghouse: A cheap place to live if you don't mind sharing a toilet with fifty other people.

Boardingschool: Where you should have sent junior before he got so out of hand.

Boastful: Usually the language of someone who has never really done anything interesting in his life.

Bodyguard: Walking bullet-proof vest.

Bogus: Infomercials.

Bomb: To misuse a restroom.

Bond: Usually not high enough.

Bondage: Fun when it's not you.

Bonfire: Your car if the party gets out of hand.

Bonus: Something you are likely to be cheated out of by management before the end of the year.

Bookkeeper: Someone who watches your money who needs to be watched himself.

Boor: The guy next to you at the bar.

Bootleg: That shitty DVD you bought on the street corner that has babies crying in the background and the shadows across the screen of people going to the bathroom and getting popcorn.

Booze: What the boor next to you at the bar is full of.

Boot: What you'd like to stick in the ass of the boor next to you at the bar.

Booty: When properly cared for, a work of art.

Borrow: How you lose most of your power tools.

Bottomless: Any friend's stomach when you are buying.

Boulevard: Where Dad gets arrested on Saturday night.

Bowling: Sport for old folks and kids (harder than it looks).

Boxing: Getting your brain damaged for large sums of money.

Boy Scout: The kid who charges $60.00 for a box of popcorn.

Brain: The most neglected of the bodily organs.

Brainless: How most people go through life.

Brat: Everyone else's child.

Brave: A way to be that is seriously lacking in today's society.

Breakdown: Likely to happen after twenty years on the job and all you get is a clock.

Breakup: An occurrence you try to avoid unless you get to do it first.

Breakwater: Farting in the tub.

Breast: The object of male visual attention.

Breast-feeding: Something that Dad would probably enjoy just as much as the baby does.

Breathe: Hard to do in the smoking area of a restaurant.

Breeding: Happens less often if the party is chaperoned.

Brew: What Grandpa uses the bathtub to do.

Bribe: The easiest way to get past a zoning commission.

Bride: A very nervous woman at a wedding.

Bridegroom: The guy with the shotgun in his back at a wedding.

Bridesmaid: The woman who will bite your eyes out for the bouquet at a wedding.

Brief: What no meeting ever is.

Broccoli: A substance that is hard to get your child to eat once some other child brainwashes him by telling him he doesn't like vegetables.

Bronze: What you do with old baby shoes to make them harder to throw away.

Broom: Cat repellant.

Brothel: Good business.

Brother: A sibling famous for stealing off of your plate, tearing up your homework and blaming you for things that he broke.

Browbeat: What police do when they interrogate (similar to how a wife interrogates).

Brownie: A point earned by sucking up to the boss.

Brownish: The noses of your coworkers.

Brussels sprouts: A good way to make children cry at the table.

Bubble: What you call a fart from a little kid to make it sound cute.

Buccaneer: A car salesman.

Budget: Usually not as tight as it should be.

Buffet: A restaurant that allows you to make a pig of yourself.

Buffoon: How most of us act at the buffet.

Bulge: Your stomach when you let your belt out.

Bully: In my experience: most social workers.

Bumpkin: Your toothless uncle.

Bureaucracy: Legal bullshit.

Burial: So expensive it's worth staying alive.

Bus: A human sardine can.

Busybody: Any neighbor when it comes to your personal business.

Butt: A well-rounded protrusion of the posterior.

Butter: What the above will be described as when it is *very* well rounded.

Buttermilk: A flawless example of the above.

Buzzard: A poor example.

Bystander: Not as innocent as you would think.

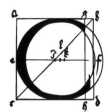

Cable: Paying for extra commercials and worthless programming.

Caddie: Usually knows more than the golfer.

Cadet: Really gung-ho until they see real combat.

Cafeteria: Where some of the worst food is.

Caffeine: What half of America is running on when they have no nicotine or alcohol.

Calculator: The downfall of people's ability to do math in their heads.

Calligraphy: A beautiful art form that has lost its value since computers have so many fonts.

Calisthenics: Doesn't do much for fat kids when it's twice a week for five minutes in public school.

Calorie: Not as key to weight loss as you have been led to believe.

Camera: Never one nearby when you need it.

Camouflage: Kind of pointless when it's orange or pink, don't you think?

Camp: When Dad makes you go out in the woods and freeze your ass off in a damp tent all night only to wake up and find out that a bear ate all your provisions.

Campaign: A questionable use of tax dollars.

Cancer: More preventable than curable.

Candy: Makes up more of a child's diet than it should.

Cannibal: Takes the concept of trying new foods a little too far.

Cap: Since when did these things start costing around $30?

Capable: A far cry from reliable.

Capacity: Can be exceeded by a single person in some cases.

Capital: Where all the behind-the-curtain action is.

Captain: Only as important as the size of the ship.

Captive: Only as important as the captor.

Caramel: Burnt sugar (did you know that?).

Carat: To some, love can be measured by it (but not to me).

Card: Sucks when it's all you get for birthday or Christmas.

Cardboard: What inner city apartments appear to be made of.

Career: All too often, it's more important to a person than anything else.

Careless: What the above-mentioned person is.

Cargo: Boxes coming in from other countries that should probably be individually inspected by a dog.

Caricature: More realistic in metaphor than in appearance.

Carnival: Where wanted men on the run find work.

Carob: Bogus chocolate.

Caroling: Not as cute in real life as it is on TV.

Carpetbagger: About nine out of ten political candidates.

Cash: The only way to pay.

Cashier: The modern equivalent of a serf.

Casino: How the white man finally tamed the Native Indian.

Caste: Used in a more subtle way in industrialized countries so as not to be noticed.

Castle: If every man is the king of one, then it's not as grand as I've heard.

Castrate: What you do when your boyfriend proposes to you in an extravagant way in front of loads of friends and relatives and you say no.

Casual: The more you try to look this way, the less you look this way.

Cat: One of the only creatures on Earth that will love you unconditionally, (when it wants to).

Catalogue: A booklet that is sent to clog your mailbox.

Catheter: A good way to have every fantasy about nurses ruined for life.

Cattle: You should thank your stars that these animals are so dumb; otherwise, they would have revolted and overthrown human society by now.

Cauliflower: Albino broccoli.

Cave: The first condo.

Cavern: The first apartment complex.

Celebrity: Sometimes this is someone who is famous because he or she is important; other times, it's someone who just thinks that they are.

Cell: More expensive than a condo but not where you want to spend your retirement.

Cell phone: A device that gives you the ability to talk to yourself in public without looking crazy.

Censorship: Robbing an idea.

Cereal: Sometimes the only way you can get kids to have some milk.

Certificate: Often as fake as whatever it's certifying.

Cesspool: Motel pool.

Chairman: A title you can obtain through a generous charity contribution.

Chambermaid: Bed-warmer (if you're lucky).

Champion: Today there are many of you, but you are seldom found to be true.

Championship: Watch it live on pay-per-view.

Chapter: Much too long if in a college text.

Character: Often mistaken for being a real person.

Charge: How you pay for things on Christmas.

Charity: An organization that sometimes is successful in ripping off both you and the person you are supposed to be helping at the same time.

Charlatan: Some TV ministries have one as a host.

Chastity: Something public school tries to sell that the students don't buy.

Cheap: Human labor.

Cheek: Jesus may have wanted you to turn the other one, but remember, you only have two...

Cheese: Good from a cow but not from your toes.

Chemically: The best way to describe how some people are imbalanced.

Cherry: If you think busting one is a sport then you are a real bastard.

Chew: When you do this, it works better if your mouth is *closed*!

Child: A little person whose achievements we should encourage instead of being jealous of them.

Childbirth: A once-in-a-lifetime experience no matter how many times you've seen it.

Childish: Most adults.

Chill: The last word you want to hear when you're upset or excited.

China: Where almost everything in the local dollar store came from.

Chink: What you call Chinese people if you want your ass kicked.

Chivalry: Dead.

Chlorine: If used in the right amount, this can keep the neighbors out of the pool by making their eyes burn.

Chocolate: Can be better than sex.

Choice: One of our greatest gifts from God that we hardly ever use.

Chopsticks: Utensils used by Asians to make us feel stupid.

Christmas: A yearly event we have been trained to celebrate by attempting to buy love.

Chubby: A word to describe the girth of your blind date delicately.

Church: A wise man once said it was in my heart, but then if it was there would be no profit in it for all those church leaders.

Cigar: Used to hide weed.

Cigarette: Something most would fight to the death for, if it wasn't already killing them.

Circulation: For most people, a bodily system that contains more lard and vegetable oil than blood.

Circumcision: Makes an ugly thing less ugly.

Circus: A show featuring people who exploit and torment animals on the road as opposed to just keeping them in one place like a zoo.

Citizenship: Worthless since just anyone can jump a border and find a job and a residence.

Civilization: Not all it's cracked up to be.

Clap: Found in your lap.

Clapper: Not a good thing to have on the lights when you're watching a show with applause.

Claptrap: Statements made during a campaign.

Classify: What the government does with things they don't want you to find out about.

Cleavage: The more you show there, the more men will stare.

Cliché: Most of what you hear in daytime drama.

Climax: What the guy usually does before you have the chance.

Clown: Scary as hell, these are for children? Whose idea was this?

Club: What I would probably use if a clown ran up to me.

Clubhouse: When you're a kid, a cardboard box makes a great one.

Clublaw: How many governments worldwide handle their people, which is why no matter how bad it may seem here, you should still count yourself lucky.

Clump: What your hair turns into in the drain.

Clumsy: The average man.

Clutch: What the average man does with his dick at every opportunity.

Cluttered: The state of the average single man's apartment.

Coast guard: This is a lot cooler of a job than the other armed services let on.

Cocaine: Something that gets more expensive the more you use it, until it uses you.

Cockfight: A kind of fight that takes on a whole new meaning when it's two guys.

Cockroach: Kind of like relatives that stop by and won't leave, except that you get to kill them.

Cocktail: One of the things casinos give you for free to try to keep you from leaving.

Coercion: Used in a police interrogation.

Coffee: Something that stains your teeth, upsets your stomach and tastes so bad you need to dump sugar, cream, milk and a ton of sweeteners and flavors in it in order to swallow it, yet everyone wants to drink the shit.

Cogitation: A state that drives me in my madness.

Cogitative: Another gift from God that we waste profusely.

Comeback: Never one handy when you need it.

Communication: With so much of this going on, why is there never enough when it counts?

Commute: Spending hours getting to and from a job you can't stand.

Company: Businessmen collectively wreaking havoc on society through advertising and cheap labor.

Comparison: Something a woman does to make a connection between you and her ex that wouldn't have existed otherwise.

Compassion: What most people should have instead.

Compatibility: Something you should look into before you sleep together.

Compensation: If you are entitled to it, how come you have to fight so damn hard to get it?

Competence: Only as good as the pay.

Competitive: Feeling this way is what keeps us ahead.

Complain: When you do this at work, you set yourself up to be fired.

Complaint: Only legitimate if you can back it up legally.

Complete: What few people feel in life.

Complex: Most relationships.

Complicate: The bullshit people do to make relationships complex.

Compliment: One of these once in a while would relieve some of the above-mentioned complication.

Complimentary: Usually, this is not anything worth your trouble.

Comprehend: Something that some people just can't seem to do, no matter how many times you explain it.

Compress: Fun with a dumpster.

Compromise: Coming to an agreement, usually by force.

Compulsive: Most dirty little habits.

Computer: Big overgrown calculator.

Con: Usually associated with the term "ex;" often used to describe a father who has been away for a while.

Concede: You can get a political candidate to do this if you are rich or clever enough.

Conceit: This applies to such a broad category of people I wouldn't even know where to begin.

Conceited: Someone who has the nerve to write a sarcastic dictionary (oops…).

Conceive: This is generally done by accident.

Concentrate: Something that gets harder to do the more someone tells you to do it.

Conception: The most trivialized miracle I know.

Concert: Must be where you go to hear screaming, because you sure can't hear the music.

Conclusion: Usually drawn on you before any facts are known.

Concrete: Makes for a very poor pair of shoes.

Concubine: I think I need me one of these.

Condescending: What you are being when you agree with idiots because they are rich and or famous.

Condom: Something you and your partner wouldn't need if you hadn't been around the block so many times.

Condominium: Another word for "stuck with your crappy apartment for life."

Condone: What is done toward the offenses of most minors.

Cone: Ice cream is messier when it comes in one of these.

Confession: Dumping your problem off on some priest instead of taking responsibility for yourself.

Confidence: What people often have more in voice than in action.

Confirmation: You should have this before believing anything anyone tells you no matter what.

Confiscation: The result of missing your furniture rental payments.

Conform: What we end up doing while we are being told to be ourselves.

Confused: How conforming leaves people with regard to their role in life.

Congeal: What all the crap you eat does in your arteries.

Congratulate: What you do to the winner before you bad-mouth him behind his back.

Congress: Where congressmen get money for nothing and the chicks for free.

Conscience: That little voice in your head that you ignore.

Consequence: People would have more self discipline if one of these followed each of their actions.

Conservation: Could work if there were any profit in it.

Consideration: Something we could give if we could get over ourselves long enough.

Consolidation: Firing a whole bunch of people.

Conspiracy: Probably more of these are true than we would ever want to know about.

Constipation: Being full of it in the physical sense as well as with ego.

Constitution: The portrait of Dorian Grey.

Constructive: The opposite of most daily activities.

Consultation: You should have many of these before committing to anything medical.

Consumer: A TV-hypnotized sucker.

Contagious: What most hands are, especially men's since they hardly ever wash after using the bathroom.

Contamination: Talking to someone with bad breath.

Contender: Who this is, is based more on money than skill.

Continuous: Most daily bullshit when you are the one who has to deal with it.

Contortionist: My dream date.

Contraband: The contents of the average glove compartment.

Contractor: Someone who makes next to nothing after being forced to keep underbidding himself.

Contradict: What people usually do to anything they have said with any moral value.

Contribution: Not likely to happen unless it's tax deductible.

Control: What is often fought over in relationships but not wanted once it's taken.

Controversial: Things that are considered this are usually not so much of a big deal in the end.

Convenience: Making easy more important than right.

Conversation: Generally gossip and lies.

Convertible: Really cool until you get caught in the rain or some kid knifes your top.

Convict: A person whose name is probably tattooed on some young girl who has an infant or is pregnant.

Convincing: What a convict has to be to get his tattooed young girl to wait for him and keep making money.

Cool: What all the convict's poorly educated, self-righteous street friends are convinced he is for being locked up, even though they can't be bothered to make calls or visit him, which sucks since he is probably in there because of them in the first place.

Cooperate: What the convict is trying not to do with his cell mates for as long as he can hold out.

Corduroy: Can start a fire depending on the thickness of her legs.

Corn: Comes out the same way it goes in.

Corn syrup: Possibly the real reason why so many Americans are obese (look into it).

Cornucopia: What we could provide the world if we weren't so wasteful.

Corporal: Not a popular punishment anymore, but it worked better than we care to admit.

Corrective: What corporal punishment was in moderation.

Correspond: Back when we used to write letters before e-mail and IM.

Corrupt: What the concept of instant mail and messaging is slowly becoming.

Corset: Uncomfortable but sexy.

Cosmopolitan: What the human race could have been by now if we could learn to cooperate.

Costly: Having a girlfriend.

Costume: Wish I could wear one every day.

Counselor: The last person you want to talk to if you're having trouble at school.

Countercharm: Announcing to your date that you don't have your wallet *after* dinner is finished.

Counterfeit: It's nearly impossible to do now, but what's the difference, money today all looks fake anyway.

Couple: Literally a pair of anything with our modern debauchery.

Coupon: The best thing to have when you shop.

Courage: Runs out for most when it's time to put your money where your mouth is.

Court: Likely wasting your time and taxpayer money so you can get screwed over.

Courteous: What you have to be to the judge when you're in court, even though he gets to be a dick to you.

Courtship: Nowadays it's fast food, a movie and the back of your car.

Cousin: Not for marrying no matter what you've heard.

Coward: He dies a thousand deaths, but not today.

Cowboy: A tall thin dusty man who spends his time tying up cows instead of his wife.

Cower: The average person's reaction to any kind of danger.

Crab: Good in salad, not in underwear.

Crack: Crabs are not good here either.

Cram: How you got the crabs.

Cramp: What you had after you got the crabs.

Cramped: The back seat of the car you got your cramp in.

Crank: A call people think is funny up until they get caught.

Cranky: Something the elderly are entitled to be after dealing with crap as long as they have.

Crater: What you'll see on the face of a teenager.

Craven: Most big-mouthed street hoods in the end.

Craving: I get one of these for ice cream just about every day.

Crayon: Half are for writing and half are for eating (just ask any four year old).

Crazy: What I am when I'm not stupid.

Creak: What gives you away when you sneak into the kitchen at two in the morning.

Cream: Supermilk.

Creative: What the right woman can inspire you to be.

Credit card: An invention that allows for you to pay for everything twice.

Creep: Little brother.

Creepy: The boys who ask you out for prom.

Crib: Used to be for babies.

Crime: Something that if it paid, you wouldn't have to keep doing it.

Cripple: Not politically correct.

Critic: Someone who has no talent, whose job is scrutinizing people who do.

Criticism: Something no one wants to hear whether it's constructive or not.

Crocodile: They wrestle you for food; you wrestle them for handbags.

Crossbreed: Everyone in a few more years.

Crossroads: A point at which we often take the wrong turn when we reach it in life.

Crotch: Bad place for an itch.

Crowbar: Master key.

Crowded: Every place you are trying to be.

Crown prince: My son–to-be.

Cruel: The dating game.

Crutch: What your boyfriend uses you for.

Cry: What you do when your boyfriend uses you as a crutch instead of pulling out from under him and letting him fall on his worthless ass.

Cubicle: Your own private hell.

Cuckold: Someone you had better pray doesn't have a gun.

Cuddle: Fun if some of you guys would give it a chance.

Cult: What most religions truly are.

Cultured: A state of existence that gives you the self-imposed right to look down your nose at anyone who has less.

Cunnilingus: Something most guys suck at (pun intended).

Cupid: Bastard.

Curb: Where you get kicked to the first time some underwear that isn't your girlfriend's ends up in her wash.

Curfew: Something many are opposed to because they don't want their kid's home anyway.

Currency: Makes the world go round.

Curse: Only bad if you hear your kid say it--never mind he heard it from you.

Custodial: If you mean child custody, then it's how to get a check for nothing.

Customers: They are always wrong; you just tell them they are always right to shut them up.

Cutthroat: How you sometimes wish you could deal with customers.

Daily: How often I wish I lived on another planet.

Dainty: How a woman can act to really piss me off.

Damnation: A career in the porno industry.

Damp: Not a good way to find your socks.

Dampness: Not something you want in your mattress.

Dance: Something that you ought not to do without knowing how.

Dancer: A lot less queer if it's a woman (stereotypically).

Dandelion: What you call a male dancer.

Dandy: What they call a male dancer in England.

Dandyish: What they call a male dancer if they haven't seen him dance yet.

Dangerous: Calling a male dancer the above things.

Dangle: What you do without Viagra.

Dangler: Grandpa.

Daredevil: Grandpa with Viagra.

Darwinism: Starting to look pretty feasible with so many Neanderthals wandering about.

Dashing: Your husband without your glasses.

Daughter: Who every scrubby, dirty, nasty teenage boy in town is after (better load the gun Dad).

Daydream: How I got through school.

Daylight: The last thing I want to see in the morning.

Dead: How most people feel in the morning.

Deadly: How most people's breath is in the morning.

Deaf: What that new car stereo system you spent so much on is making you.

Dealer: A vulture.

Death: A dealer's reward.

Debatable: Just about anything.

Debt: The ruin of us all.

Decapitate: What doctors do in a sex change operation.

Deceitful: Campaign promises.

Decency: Something totally missing in music videos.

Decipher: What needs to be done with the language on many music videos.

Decision: Will be made for you if you can't do it yourself.

Decline: The outcome of the average credit card application.

Dedicate: To put attention on someone who probably doesn't want or deserve it.

Deductible: Not as much as you think until it's too late.

Deep: What the shit is when someone else is shoveling it.

Deer: An animal that really, *really* hates your front bumper.

Defect: Most new products come with one of these, standard.

Defend: To not take any shit.

Defendant: You, explaining why you don't take any shit.

Defenseless: What you truly are if you are defending yourself with the above attitude.

Defensive: How you act when you did something that you know you was wrong.

Deficit: What the national budget usually has.

Deflower: Something that happens way too early.

Deformed: What you fear your blind date will be.

Degenerate: What your blind date was instead of deformed.

Delegate: To stick someone else with your nasty job.

Delete: What people accidentally do to your files when they use your computer.

Deliberate: What the above-mentioned deletion actually was.

Delicious: A common nickname for a gay man.

Delinquency: A teenage pastime.

Delusion: A state in which many of us live.

Demand: What I am not likely to comply with.

Democracy: Not all it's cracked up to be.

Democrat: Someone who claims allegiance to democracy, while often seeming to not understand the nature of it.

Demon: What many Democrats act like.

Demoralize: What Democrats seek to do to the other political parties instead of working with them, which would be the democratic thing to do.

Denial: The state Democrats would be in if you accused them of any of the above.

Dentist: A man with hairy arms and bad teeth who sticks his hands in your mouth.

Denture: The main reason you should never drink from a glass sitting on someone's nightstand.

Deodorant: A cosmetic that comes in two varieties: too strong or not strong enough.

Deplete: What a woman does to your bank account as soon as she gets comfortable.

Deplorable: What the above-mentioned kind of behavior is.

Deportation: Sending South Americans back for a quick vacation before they return to the States.

Depression: Fuel for artists and writers.

Deserving: Something people think they are, especially when they are not.

Desire: Wanting what you can't have.

Desist: What you need to do with any action arising from those desires.

Despair: The state you will fall into if you don't desist from the actions arising from your desires.

Desperation: How most of us end up with our jobs.

Despicable: The jobs we end up with.

Despot: The boss.

Destiny: Cruel if it's true.

Detention: A popular after-school activity.

Develop: Something your daughter does to make you nervous.

Device: A secret your wife keeps in her dresser for after you fall asleep.

Diabolical: The truth behind most political decisions.

Diaper: A really creepy fetish.

Diarrhea: Your reward for not sticking to a proper diet.

Diary: A book in which you record the lies you tell yourself.

Dictatorship: Owning your own business.

Dictionary: What this book is an insult to.

Diet: What everyone does but does wrong.

Different: Something you can be and it is OK (in theory).

Difficult: How it is to be different.

Digestible: Most things that you shouldn't eat.

Dignify: What you shouldn't do to most accusations by answering them.

Dildo: What the secret device in the draw was.

Dilute: What the ice is for at a bar.

Diploma: Often not worth the paper it's written on.

Diplomacy: A profession where you strike nasty little deals with other countries.

Diplomat: Usually an evil little bastard.

Dire: Any situation after a group of these diplomats have been meeting in secret.

Dirty: Money and underwear.

Disability: Often faked for profit.

Disadvantage: What people with real problems are left at after everyone else has ripped off the disability programs.

Disagreement: Can get you killed.

Disappear: Something I wish I could do.

Disappointment: Oddly enough, what many people feel after they have gotten what they wanted.

Disbelief: What people would react with if you tried to explain the above description.

Disc: Got rid of vinyl.

Discharge: Very nasty no matter where it came from.

Disciple: A professional loser.

Discipline: What it wouldn't kill American parents to try on their children.

Disclaimer: Really small fine print that keeps companies from getting sued over consumer stupidity.

Disconnect: What I do to telemarketers.

Discount: Comes with five fingers.

Discourage: What all those fake cameras in department stores are supposed to do to shoplifters.

Discredit: The job of a campaign manager.

Discreet: Classy prostitutes.

Discrimination: Often works in reverse.

Disgraceful: How Americans are represented in other countries because of certain policies and business practices.

Disguise: What many of us have to travel in because of the above-mentioned policies and practices.

Dishonest: What foreigners consider us to be.

Disloyal: Often the people you trust the most.

Disorder: What a company puts their records in if they are in any sort of trouble.

Dispatch: The more you need them the slower they are.

Disperse: Works better with teargas.

Dispossession: Your reward for cheating on your income tax.

Disproportion: What most stories people tell about themselves are done in.

Dispute: What the above-mentioned people do when other people tell tall tales.

Disrespect: What you are doing to yourself when you lie to build yourself up.

Disrobe: Something fun to watch (when it's the opposite sex).

Dissatisfaction: What many experience after the honeymoon.

Dissect: Why most people don't like biology.

Distance: What you don't have enough of when someone is talking to you with bad breath.

Distasteful: Whatever the person with bad breath must have eaten.

Distillation: The proper verb form of "running the still."

Distraction: Just about anything can be one of these if you don't like what you are doing.

Distressing: Shopping for the holidays.

Distrustful: Any company's loss prevention division.

Ditto: What you should never say when someone says "I love you."

Divide: Something many states force you to do with property after divorce.

Divorce: How a woman gets to take all of your stuff and get paid for doing it.

Divulge: What your ex-wife does with all of your personal business during the divorce.

Document: What you should do with all of your property to avoid the above-mentioned division.

Documentary: Probably the only valuable kinds of shows on television.

Dog: Any boyfriend who introduces you as his bitch.

Doll: Not the same if it's inflatable.

Dollar: The most useless thing people kill and die for.

Domestic: What all animals will eventually end up being.

Dominant: The most foolish and wasteful species on Earth.

Domination: Not my bag.

Donation: Doesn't always end up where you think.

Donor: A huge source of income for major hospitals.

Doomsday: Always seems to be around the corner but never comes.

Doorknob: Often used as an explanation for a black eye.

Dormitory: A college residence where it seems to be OK to violate every rule in the book.

Double-dealing: Your average deal.

Double-life: Dad's life between leaving work and arriving home late.

Douche: The guy at work who rats out every shortcut you take on the job.

Downhill: Where life seems to go once you slip the first time.

Downtrodden: What you are when you hit the bottom.

Dozen: Doughnuts are better when they come this way.

Drama: Something that there is so much of in people's lives it doesn't make any sense to me why they want to watch it on TV.

Drastic: The measures people with no money will go to, to get some.

Drawback: That taking drastic measures to get money is a good way to end up in jail.

Dreadful: The conditions you will find once you are in jail.

Dream: Often better than reality.

Dreamer: Some of the best and most suppressed minds.

Dreamless: The people doing the suppressing of the dreamers.

Drinkable: In many countries, only the hotel water.

Drudge: How you get through a day at work.

Drug: What Mom uses to get through life.

Drunk: How Dad gets through life.

Dude: Not so flattering a nickname if you know the true definition.

Dull: Cable TV.

Dummy: What I feel like when I sit in front of a TV.

Dung: What I feel like my head is full of when I sit in front of a TV.

Dupe: What the advertisers on TV think I am.

Dusty: Your wife's pussy.

Dwarfish: Your husband's penis.

Dynamite: My penis.

Eagle: A large, magnificent bird of prey that has its wings clipped and is kept in a tiny cage for your viewing pleasure.

Eardrum: A part of the ear that you are shredding with your car stereo.

Earring: An ornamentation that just doesn't look right on a guy.

Earth: Our own personal garbage dump.

Earthling: Something I wish I wasn't sometimes.

Earthquake: What God uses to punish California.

Easter: A holiday that would have us believe that chocolate bunnies who lay colored eggs have something to do with Christ.

Easy: The opposite of everything in life.

Eavesdrop: What people do when you ask for privacy.

Eccentric: What every genius seems before you realize how smart he is.

Echo: How you know you are too damn loud.

Ecstasy: Hopefully, the state of my next relationship.

Eczema: Full body dandruff.

Eden: Really, the whole Earth before we messed it up.

Edit: The act of ruining a body of writing.

Editor: Probably the only person to get the above definition.

Education: In this country, it's a fraud.

Educator: Someone who is fooling himself if involved with public education.

Efficiency: Something that cannot be achieved without close supervision.

Egotism: What the mass media and advertising teach the young.

Ejaculation: Embarrassing, when it happens early.

Elaborate: Impossible for a child to do when you want him to explain something.

Election: When politicians show you who they want you to vote for.

Electrician: A person you pay a fortune to for playing around with something that looks so simple you would think a child could do it.

Electrocution: What happens to you when you try to do electrical work yourself because you thought it was so easy a child could do it.

Electrolysis: Electrocuting yourself on purpose.

Elevator: Scary in movies, harmless in real life.

Eligibility: Something with requirements that get harder the more you need it.

Elongation: What a penis enlarger is supposed to achieve (good luck getting it to work).

Elsewhere: Where I wish I were every time the phone rings.

Emasculated: How you feel when you get a dressing down from your girl in public.

Emasculating: Catching your wife with another woman, and you are *not* invited.

Embarrassment: What you would think most parents would feel when their kids act like barbarians in the local market.

Embezzle: How you give yourself a bonus.

Embryo: More alive than you think.

Emission: A polite description for when you cut the mustard.

Emotional: Any pregnant woman.

Emperor: What I would like my next job to be.

Empire: What I would like my next community to be.

Employment: Not all it's cracked up to be, (we were better off on farms).

Enchant: What strippers do.

Enchantress: Goal-digger.

Encroach: The Patriot Act does it.

Encyclopedia: Used to fill a bookshelf, now it comes on a disc.

Endanger: What people do to their children when leaving them in many daycares.

Endless: Infomercials.

Endorsement: What an athlete can't get by without anymore.

Endowment: How companies sneak commercials onto non-commercial television.

Enema: Wrong. It's just wrong.

Enemy: What almost every other country seems to consider the U.S. to be.

Enfeeble: What you do when you to old folks when you put them in eldercare facilities.

Enforce: A function that seems to be impossible for unpopular laws.

Engaged: What you are when you spend too much on a ring that you can't get back if she changes her mind.

English: A language that is spoken fluently and with excellent grammar in every country on Earth except for America.

Enhance: What has to be done to the computer system that you just bought after you get it home.

Enigma: Any answers to a question at a press conference.

Enjoyment: The goal of someone perpetrating solicitation.

Enlargement: A prostitute's goal.

Enlist: A recruitment officer's goal.

Enrollment: A college's goal.

Enslavement: Your husband's goal.

Ensnarement: Your company's goal.

Entertainment: The guy at the strip club's goal.

Enticement: The stripper's goal.

Entombment: Your wife's goal if she catches you with the strippers again.

Environment: A lot more fragile than you think.

Envy: A human illness.

Epicure: What you become when you win the lottery.

Epidemic: What breaks out *after* they administer flu shots.

Epithalamium: Something that never seems to come out right when it's time.

Equality: Harder to reach than you think.

Equestrian: Glorified pony rider.

Equivalent: What you don't want when the market runs out of the sale item.

Eraser: What the teacher makes you pound to choke you with chalk dust.

Erection: Something that, if it still works when you're old, you're happy.

Erotica: The nicer form of porno.

Eruption: Teenage acne.

Escalade: It used to mean breaking into a castle.

Escalator: What you use when you are too lazy for stairs.

Escort: Expensive prostitute.

Espionage: Selling out.

Essay: A paper with which you are judged on how boring you are.

Essential: Nowadays, a home theatre system.

Eternity: The line at the post office.

Ethics: They have a class for this in college (no one told them you can't learn this from a book).

Etiquette: Something that would do the world a great favor if people bothered to teach it to their children anymore.

Eulogy: Usually a lot of lies.

European: A chain smoker with bad teeth and a worse economy.

Evaluation: The excuse your company uses not to promote you.

Evangelist: All too often a con artist.

Even-handed: What I wish the court system was.

Everlasting: What love should be.

Eviction: The reward for skipping rent.

Evidence: Something that can still bury you even if it doesn't hold water.

Evil: A state of mind for many.

Evolution: A natural function that seems to be going backwards for the human race.

Exaggeration: Any story that anyone tells you that is even half interesting.

Example: Something that most parents don't set very well anymore.

Excellence: What we should be trying to get our children to strive for.

Exchangeable: Anything you bought if you lost the receipt.

Exciting: Any carnival ride that doesn't make you sick.

Excommunicate: What the pope does if you piss him off.

Excrement: Fancy word for shit.

Excruciating: College lectures.

Execution: Pink slip.

Executive: Executor.

Executrix: If the executive is a gal.

Exempt: What a multi-billion-dollar company is when it breaks the law).

Exercise: Fast becoming taboo in many industrialized countries.

Exhausted: What people are if they try the above-mentioned exercise.

Exhume: Undoing what shouldn't be.

Exorcism: Many teenagers seem to need one.

Exoskeleton: What your clothes turn into after you've worn them consecutively for several days.

Exotic: What a relationship should be.

Expectation: Often a letdown.

Expeditious: The opposite of what postal service is.

Expel: Not as much of a threat to a teenager as you may have been led to believe.

Expensive: Women.

Experience: How you learn about the above.

Expert: No such thing when it comes to relationships.

Explanation: There's never a good enough one of these for cheating.

Exploitation: Pimping.

Expressionless: A victim of Botox.

Expropriate: What's done with drug money.

Expunge: What happens to your social status when you get life in prison.

Exquisite: The pain associated with depression.

Exterior: The main concern of most individuals who have lost focus on what's really important.

Extermination: The secret goal of most countries (in reference to their neighbors).

Exterritorial: If your country has the money, this is where their laws also apply.

Extinct: Table manners, decent language, family entertainment, etc.

Extortion: A business of such magnitude it's a wonder that it's not listed on the stock exchange.

Extra: Something you can't have if you can't pay for it.

Extraordinary: The level of how much you can get away with when your company has a government contract.

Extravaganza: What any court case turns into when you are a celebrity.

Exuberant: Your lifestyle if you are a hip-hop performer.

Eyebrow: That tuft of hair above your eyes that needs to be parted in the middle.

Eyesore: The neighbor's house.

Eyewitness: A person prone to keeping his mouth shut.

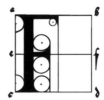

Fable: Most autobiographies.

Fabricate: To write an autobiography.

Fabulous: What people who write autobiographies think they are.

Facial: Something that only girls on the Internet are willing to take.

Facilitate: The opposite of any governing body does.

Facsimile: What the attitude is of most American youth to the attitude of anyone in a music video.

Fact: An item that is twisted out of shape by the time we hear it.

Factory: Where children find work overseas.

Fad: Back in style in ten years.

Fag: A schoolboy in England who does certain tasks for a senior (that's the actual definition-- creepy, huh?)

Fail: What a little manipulation with test scores will keep your kid from doing long enough for the school to get its funding (think about it).

Failure: Any government-enforced program that involves public education.

Fair: The opposite of how most of us get treated.

Faith: Readily available but hard to keep.

Faking: What most people who claim to have faith are doing.

Fallacy: Closing arguments in court.

Family: You get stuck with an extra one of these upon marriage (as if yours wasn't bad enough).

Famine: An situation you see in many countries that should remind us not to waste so much.

Famous: A false state of grandeur confused with popularity (real famous people: Moses, Jesus, Buddha, Muhammad; not really famous: athletes, actors, politicians, musicians, etc.)

Fan: Someone obsessed with a person they think is famous.

Fanatic: The reason celebrities have bodyguards.

Fanfaronade: Many late night talk show hosts.

Fantasy: The type of world too many of us live in instead of the real one.

Farce: The outcome of any court hearing involving a celebrity.

Farmer: A dying breed (hang in there folks).

Farming: An unappreciated profession.

Fart: A good way to make room on the bus.

Farthing: What a penny is really worth.

Fashion: More important than function.

Fast: What the drive-through is supposed to be.

Fat: What Americans are.

Fatal: What being fat is for many Americans.

Father: That guy who stops by every couple of months and argues with Mom over child support.

Fatherhood: A rarity.

Fatherless: The majority of America's youth, it seems.

Fatten: To frequent fast food restaurants.

Favoritism: How many people get promoted.

Fearful: Why you don't say anything about how the above-mentioned people got promoted.

Fearless: What you should be.

Featureless: Police sketches.

Fee: Nothing in life seems to come without one.

Feeble: Any effort to help the environment.

Feel: Often copped in the dark.

Felon: One of a very large population.

Felony: What so many have on their record that makes it hard for them to get a job.

Feminine: How most women don't act anymore (and many men do).

Fence: A barrier between neighbors that you throw your leaves over when you rake them up in the fall.

Feral: Teenagers after puberty.

Fiancé: The shackle you will be locked into.

Fiasco: The wedding.

Fidelity: What few grooms understand.

Field day: What the groom has when he isn't being watched.

Fiend: How the bride views the groom after he gets caught having a field day.

Fifteen: Can get you twenty.

Fight: Something many need little excuse to do.

Filibuster: A lobbyist.

Filth: What you find under your kid's bed.

Fire: Fun to watch (unless it's your house).

Fired: What you are for voicing any kind of opinion on the job.

Fire engine: Really cool, if you are like five.

Fireman: Someone who doesn't get as much respect as he should.

First-class: Airline seats for which you are overcharged.

Fishing: Incredibly boring, especially on television.

Fixation: What a male has pertaining to dirty magazines.

Flame: To act really, really gay.

Flatulence: Farting with style.

Flaunt: What many do in front of the loser.

Flawless: Nature as opposed to manmade.

Fleece: To sell stock.

Flexible: The best kind of girlfriend.

Flimsy: American or Chinese products made in mass production.

Flirt: Still cheating.

Flower: A beautiful thing that you kill to be romantic.

Flowery: What the uncle who no one talks about is.

Flunky: Dad when Mom wears the pants.

Flush: What stupid people do over and over after the toilet clogs the first time.

Flypaper: Sticks your hair more than it catches flies.

Foggy: Grandpa's memory.

Follower: Sucker.

Fondle: First base (or is that second?).

Food: Makes up a huge percentage of American garbage.

Foodio: It's foodio, you know, foodio foodio foodio (private joke for Danielle).

Foolish: What we are for throwing away so much food.

Footstool: Any assistant to an executive.

Forbidden: Most teenage activities.

Foreigner: The person who does the jobs that you won't.

Forensics: Could have kept a lot of innocent people out of jail if invented earlier.

Foreplay: Something your husband just doesn't understand.

Forest: Fodder for paper mills.

Forget: What people tend to do after they've done something wrong.

Forgiveness: Nearly impossible for most people.

Formality: Red tape.

Formerly: Unemployed.

Fornication: The hobby of many husbands.

Forsake: What many husbands do to their vows.

Forswear: What many husbands do when they are caught forsaking their vows.

Fortitude: What the above-mentioned husbands must have to be so bold.

Fortunate: What the above-mentioned husbands are if their wives buy their stories.

Fortune: What the above-mentioned husbands will lose if their wives take them to court.

Fortune-teller: Con artist.

Fossilize: What you do while you stand in the customer service line at the department store.

Foul-mouthed: Children after attending school.

Frame: To blame the other guy.

France: One of the few countries that can boast that it has defeated itself in many combat situations throughout history.

Fraudulent: Your average e-mail.

Freak: The guy who wrote the fraudulent e-mail named above.

Freakish: Any brother to any sister.

Free: A lie.

Freeborn: The only time you are free.

Freedom: One of the most difficult states of being to achieve.

Free will: Good luck with this one.

French: What you call a citizen of a country where you can get away with being terribly rude (actually that sounds kind of neat).

Fresh: A word that people into hip-hop don't want to hear anymore.

Freshman: This year is as far as most people get in college.

Friction: Obtainable in the bedroom.

Friend: Very few of these truly exist.

Friendship: Something that doesn't come without a price.

Frigid: Your wife after you say, "I do."

Frisking: It can be awkward or fun depending on who is doing it.

Frivolous: TV shows about the lives of celebrities.

Frosting: Sometimes the best part of the cake (and not just for cake).

Frugal: A nice way to say "cheap."

Frump: The aunt who still gives you a Christmas card with five dollars in it even though you are thirty-two years old.

Fudge: Often packed depending on gender.

Fugitive: There's one in every other house on the block.

Full-blown: Any condition with which you refuse to go to the doctor.

Fume: What Dad does as he does the taxes.

Fumigation: What the bathroom seems to need every time you go in after someone else.

Fun: The opposite of school.

Funambulist: A single mother with four or more children.

Fundamental: What reading is supposed to be.

Funeral: Can be a good thing if the person was disliked.

Fungus: Gym socks.

Funnel: That thing you never seem to have when you need to add oil.

Funny: The opposite of most stand-up comics.

Fur: Seems to be popular if it's fake.

Furlough: A privilege that combat soldiers should get more of.

Furtive: Some of the best ideas.

Fuss: What you make when you can't let something go.

Futile: Menial labor jobs.

Future: What many people with menial labor jobs do not have.

Fuzzy: The memory of anyone being interrogated.

Gadget: Any electronic device to Grandpa when he doesn't know what the hell it is.

Gaelic: English that's so hard to understand that only the Scots can decipher it.

Gag: There should be one of these for every five year old's mouth.

Galaxy: A very good reminder of how small we really are.

Gallant: What every young lady on a blind date hopes the guy is until her dreams are crushed upon opening the door.

Gallery: Recently used to display trash and finger-painting.

Galley slave: Newbie in the Navy.

Gamble: To waste your money.

Gambler: To waste your life.

Gangster: Self glorified thug.

Garage: Where you store everything else but your car.

Garbage: What is usually in the garage with everything else.

Gardener: A Mexican, (stereotypically).

Garish: Clothing worn to the Oscars.

Garlic: A good defense against talent agents.

Gas: Still cheaper than a gallon of milk (so quit your bitching).

Gas mask: A good defense against diapers.

Gasp: What you do when you smell diapers and you don't have the gas mask.

Gaudy: Clothing worn to the Emmy awards.

Gay: Merry, animated, frolicsome, happy, quick (this is the actual definition, which is funny enough by itself).

Geld: Very painful indeed.

Gender: Apparently very confusing for some folk.

Generic: The only food most people can afford without a coupon.

Genitals: Teabags.

Gentleman: Something young men ought to get lessons on becoming.

Geography: A subject often failed by high school students.

Gerrymander: Something that happens in most elections worldwide.

Ghastly: What a woman looks like after a Botox treatment.

Ghetto: Once upon a time if you looked in the dictionary it would say a Jewish neighborhood (my how things have changed).

Gibberish: Ebonics.

Gifted: The type of person who will drown in public school.

Gin: Flavoring for Grandma's coffee.

Gingerbread: Great smelling product used to build houses that are inedible.

Gingerbread-man: Why, it's me, I'm the gingerbread-man.

Girdle: What you don't want to see Grandma in.

Glaucoma: An excuse to smoke weed.

Glorification: Any celebrity who writes his own autobiography before he's been in the business for at least ten years.

Glove: Not enough to convict.

Glowworm: An insect near a reactor.

Glue: Snack food for kindergarteners.

Gluttony: Another American pastime.

Godless: What employee benefit packages are.

Godlike: How CEOs feel when they look at their own titles.

Godsend: What every guy on a dating show thinks he is.

Gold: Worthless if it's less than 14carat.

Golf: Harder than it looks and more boring than it seems.

Good-for-nothing: Any adult still living at home who's not in college.

Good-natured: All nature.

Good will: Not always so willing and not very good.

Gordian knot: Any legal document.

Gorgeous: Me.

Gospel: Misquoted, misinterpreted and misused.

Gourmet: A cushy job.

Government: The people who waste your tax money.

Governor: A position that is apparently only important if you are in a coastal city.

Grace: Something I would like to see more young ladies with.

Graciously: How most people neglect to lose.

Graduation: An event that fewer and fewer people make it to anymore.

Grammar: Something that fewer and fewer people are able to use properly anymore.

Grandchild: All too often raised by the grandparent.

Grant: The only way most of us make it through college.

Gratification: The only thing people seem to care about anymore.

Gratuity: Something you could leave more of the next time you dine out.

Gravitate: What guys in a bar tend to do around the young lady with the D cups.

Gray: My hair after a phone call from the ex.

Greatness: Something it wouldn't kill more of us to strive for.

Greedy: How too many of us act.

Grope: An action that some young men try to sneak in on the first date.

Gross: What the young lady thinks the above-mentioned action is.

Ground: Where the young man is likely to end up when he catches one in the nuts for the above-mentioned action.

Grovel: What the above-mentioned young man is likely to do next.

Grudge: What she will carry with her for you after your date.

Grumpy: Me before 10:00 in the morning.

Guiltless: The attitude of most incarcerated people.

Guinea-pig: A really miserable pet (whose idea was this? Don't people eat these somewhere?).

Gull: Flying rat.

Gullible: What you are to advertising agencies.

Gun: It's my God-given right to have one, damnit!

Gunboat: I want one of those too!

Gunpowder: And I want some of this!

Gunshot: *Yeehawwwww!!!!!!!*

Gutter: The location of the minds of most television advertisers.

Gymnast: Ten times more of an athlete than most others, but not recognized because there's no money in the sport.

Gyneocracy: The ultimate goal of the woman's liberation movement.

Gynecology: Really cool idea for the young male medical student until they actually see what they will be dealing with.

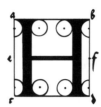

Habit: Something dirty that people do that is everyone else's fault because they can't or won't control themselves.

Habitable: The opposite of most inner city apartments.

Habitat: Really nice way of saying "animal prison."

Habitual: When someone has become a lost cause.

Hacks: Most modern writers.

Haggis: A food that was once probably eaten out of desperation (what the excuse is now, I have no idea).

Hailstone: God's way of ruining your car.

Hairdresser: A small foreign woman who talks about you in a different language with a big smile.

Half-dead: Most of us in the morning.

Half-hearted: Most of us on a job interview.

Half pay: What most of us are stuck with upon retirement, (if we're lucky).

Half-witted: The people who make the decisions about our retirement plans.

Hallucination: Fooling yourself by accident.

Halloween: When we send our kids out begging for candy, although it would have been cheaper to keep them home and buy them candy, when you consider the cost of the costumes.

Hammock: A safety bed designed to protect sailors from other sailors sneaking into bed with them (naughty sailors).

Handbook: A booklet you get when you are hired for a job that explains in detail how you are going to be screwed over.

Handcuff: A device that, if applied to you, usually means you are in for a lot of trouble or a good time.

Handful: Children.

Handicraftsmen: A dying breed.

Handmaiden: Something most grooms are expecting but seldom receive.

Handrail: What you are usually stuck with on the bus because all the seats are taken.

Handsome: Me!

Hand job: What your girlfriend eventually does to avoid third base at all costs.

Handwriting: A personal craft that is fast becoming lost amongst the youth of today as it becomes sloppier and more illegible.

Hangman: The judge in a divorce case.

Harass: What your ex is apparently entitled to do to you after you break up.

Hardheaded: Your kids.

Hardhearted: Your boss.

Hardship: Your life.

Harebrained: Your wife.

Harem: What you wish you had instead.

Harlequin: Your husband.

Harlot: What your mother-in-law secretly says your wife is.

Harmless: What most people who make violent threats are.

Harmony: What the kids in elementary school music classes lack.

Harpy: My ex.

Hashish: What your parents spent most of their time with in the '60s.

Hatred: A miserable waste of energy.

Havoc: Two minutes to the bell on Wall Street.

Hazardous: Coming home drunk at three in the morning when your wife is still up.

Headache: The result of the verbal onslaught you get for coming home drunk at three in the morning when your wife is still up.

Headstone: What you will probably be under when your wife is done (see above).

Heartbreaking: The current condition of the world.

Heartburn: What you get when you have several foods that you cannot eat but you do anyway.

Heartless: Anything involving child custody or visitation.

Heaven: Desired by most, achieved by few.

Heavy: A smoker's breathing after climbing a flight of stairs.

Hectic: Traffic at 5:20 p.m.

Hedge: Where the peeping tom hides out.

Hedonism: The secret philosophy of most people.

Heedless: What anyone you give advice to is.

Heehaw: No kidding, this is actually a real word.

Helium: A gas that, when inhaled, will make you sound as stupid as the act of inhaling the gas in the first place is.

Hell: The ultimate destination of most of the human population.

Helter-skelter: How most new laws are passed.

Hemorrhoids: What customers are (to cashiers).

Henchman: The guy who serves you with a summons.

Henpeck: What your wife does when she gives you instructions.

Herbivores: What farm animals are supposed to be, were, and should be again (unless we want more mad cow disease).

Hermaphrodite: A state of being that is now obtainable through surgery.

Hermit: The only way to get any peace and quiet anymore.

Hero: Used to refer to an incredibly brave and selfless person; now it refers to athletes, the wealthy and whoever else the media tells us.

Hiding: Something terrorist leaders are good at.

Hideous: Makeup in most teen magazines.

Highbrow: The average retired rapper.

High-strung: Small dogs.

Highwayman: Now replaced by toll booths.

Hilarious: Airport security.

History: Something we could learn from if we paid attention to it.

Hitchhiker: A person who turns his life over to a stranger on the road.

Hoarding: A pointless ritual usually performed in supermarkets in the Eastern states at the hint of a storm.

Hoaxes: What most nightly news stories are.

Hobgoblin: Nightly news reporter.

Hobnob: Sounds kinkier than it is.

Hog wash: Journalism.

Homeless: A larger population than anyone would care to admit.

Homely: A blind date.

Homesick: A college student when he goes out on his own and sees his first utility bills.

Honesty: Something so rare I can hardly recognize it anymore.

Honeydew: Your first kiss (if you're lucky).

Honeymoon: Over faster than you expected.

Honor: Seriously lacking in people for some time.

Hopeless: The state of the world if we don't do something soon.

Hormones: What directs the actions of most teenage boys.

Homosexual: A lifestyle that is more popular on TV than in real life.

Horny: The result of hormones.

Horoscope: Bullshit.

Horror: The most worthless movie category.

Horseback: Rough without a saddle.

Hostage: Anyone with a mortgage.

Hourly: The worst way to get paid.

Housekeeper: The person who goes through your luggage.

Huddle: What the family does in winter when the gas gets turned off.

Hug: Most don't get enough of these.

Human: Flawed.

Human resources: The department responsible for underpaying overqualified people.

Humane: Human beings behaving as if there were no human element.

Humiliated: How you feel walking around in your department store uniform.

Hungry: A terrible way to go to bed.

Hunter: One who uses wild game as an excuse to shoot something.

Husband: That thing on the sofa with one hand on a beer and the other in his pants.

Husky: What you politely call a child when they are fat.

Hydraulics: Really cool when they are under the car.

Hydrophobia: An excuse not to wash.

Hygiene: The average male cleverly disguises his lack of this with deodorant and cologne.

Hypnotism: The effect of music videos.

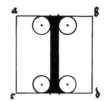

Ice: What makes up about 80 percent of your soft drink in a fast food restaurant.

Ice cream: Food of the gods; I could live off of this stuff forever (one cool point to the Arabs, sorry, not the Greeks, they made snow-cones).

Ichor: My blood type.

Ideal: The impossible dream.

Idealism: The constitution.

Identification: Don't get caught without it.

Identity: Not stolen as often as credit card companies would have you believe.

Idiosyncrasy: Sometimes can be enough to make you want to strangle someone.

Idiot: The average person in the customer service line.

Idly: How the person behind the counter is working anyway.

Idolater: A real idiot.

Igloo: Shanty for the arctic homeless.

Ignorance: It's no excuse for breaking the law, or so I'm told. But the way the law is designed, it's hard not to be.

Ignore: The best way to handle ignorant people.

Ill: Another word that hip-hop people wish wasn't being used anymore.

Ill-bred: What you would think most people are, the way we act.

Illiterate: Public school students.

Ill-mannered: Public school students.

Illogical: Public school curriculum.

Ill-tempered: Public school teachers.

Illusion: The law that governs public schools.

Illusionist: The person who writes the laws that govern public schools.

Illustrator: Usually makes more than the writer.

Ill will: What is wished on you by people who claim to forgive.

Image: What people consider the most important thing.

Imagination: A quality too many of us lack.

Imitate: Children do this to be funny (makes you want to drop kick them).

Immaculate: My house (I wish).

Immeasurable: My bank account (still wishing).

Immense: My penis (no comment).

Immoral: Prime time television.

Immortal: Still wishing.

Imp: A child you have to baby-sit.

Impassive: The Lincoln tunnel at 5:30 p.m.

Impeach: The higher the politician's rank, the harder this is to do to him.

Impeccable: How politicians look before the trial.

Impenetrable: The hottest-looking girl at the club.

Imperfect: Any attempt you make to talk to the hottest-looking girl at the club.

Impolite: Restaurant customers.

Important: A matter of opinion.

Impose: What relatives do to you when they drop by unannounced.

Impossible: What it can be to get rid of relatives once they show up.

Impoverish: What relatives can do to you if they stay too long.

Impregnable: The mean ugly girl from the debating club.

Impressionist: One of the worst kinds of comics.

Imprint: What happens to your forehead when hit by someone who wears rings.

Imprison: What happens to the guy who hits you while wearing rings if you can prove it.

Impulse: What most people act on.

Inability: What many so-called professionals actually display.

Inaccessible: Any shortcut you need in a traffic jam.

Inaccurate: Radio traffic reports.

Inadequate: Your fiancé to your parents.

Inamorata: She whom I seek.

Inane: The boss.

Inanimate: Your wife in bed.

Inappreciable: Your husband's performance in bed.

Inapproachable: Your husband in bed without a shower.

Inappropriate: What he really wants in bed.

Inbred: More of your relatives than you would care to admit.

Incapacitate: What cops on TV try to do instead of beating you're the guy's ass.

Incarceration: What comes after the cops incapacitate you.

Incense: What you use to cover up the smell of weed.

Incest: Where all those inbred relatives came from.

Inch: The size of the average penis (sorry boys).

Inch-meal: You getting oral sex.

Incognito: You at the sex shop.

Incoherent: You after a few drinks.

Incoming: The frying pan to your forehead when you come in drunk at 2:00 a.m. from the sex shop.

Inconceivable: The amount of damage your wife can do with that frying pan (see above).

Inconsiderate: You for not thinking about your wife first (that's me not wanting to cross a woman with a frying pan, see above).

Inconsistent: Any story you come up with to explain your whereabouts (see above).

Inconsolable: Your wife at her sister's afterwards (see above).

Inconvenience: Obviously, what it is to be living with you.

Incriminating: Finding a blond hair on your jacket.

Incurable: Most casino gamblers.

Indecent: The contents of commercials later in the evening.

Indian: A majority that became a minority.

Indifferent: How some Indians feel about becoming a minority.

Indignant: How the rest of the Indians feel about becoming a minority.

Individual: What I wish every teenager in America would try to be instead of copying everyone else.

Industry: Where pollution comes from.

Inebriated: What college kids are when they should be studying instead.

Inefficient: What inebriation makes college students.

Inevitable: Inebriated college students kissing the porcelain throne.

Inexcusable: What the parents of college students consider inebriation to be even though many of them probably did the same thing.

Inexhaustible: What many college kids think their parents' savings are.

Inexpensive: The real value of your engagement ring.

Inexperienced: Your new bride on the honeymoon (which can be a good thing or a bad thing depending on your preference).

Infamy: How you go down for not being popular in the media.

Infancy: The last time most of us had any purity.

Infantile: How many elementary-age kids still act.

Infatuated: How you act when watching a stripper.

Infection: What you get if you mess with a stripper.

Infidel: What we are to Arabs (stereotypically).

Inflated: The average ego.

Influence: A power that too many have.

Informer: The guy with all the perks in jail.

Ingenious: People who write dictionaries.

Ingrate: A child on Christmas morning.

Inhale: What politicians swear they didn't do.

Inheritance: The reward for putting up with all your older relative's crap.

Inhospitable: How the older relative acted whenever *you* dropped by.

Inhuman: Severe cases of the above.

Iniquity: What your older relative had that made him so intolerable.

Injection: The alternative to a good old-fashioned hanging.

Ink: Worth more than the damn printer.

Inmate: Comes with the room.

Inoperative: Used cars.

Inorganic: The produce section at the market.

In-patient: When you're this, the hospital really has its hooks in you.

Inquisition: Something I wished was still around when the church found all those molesters.

Insane: What I must be for sitting here writing this book.

Insect: An unwanted house guest.

Insecticide: How you get bugs drunk (because it sure doesn't kill them).

Insight: What I wish I had before my relationships.

Insignificant: How I was treated in my relationships.

Insomnia: What I have when I can't get over how I was treated in my relationships.

Instigator: Any little sister.

Institution: About as bad as prison.

Instrument: We should all learn to play one.

Insufferable: Listening to modern rap music.

Insulation: What I wish I had more of in the walls when the neighbor plays rap music.

Insurance: What most of us drive without.

Integrity: What you couldn't pay people to have anymore.

Intellectual: Professional smart-ass.

Intelligence: What most of us could fill a thimble with.

Intense: Me in bed.

Intercourse: A polite way to say "fucking."

Interested: What most guys are when offered the above.

Intermission: Bathroom break.

Interpretation: Usually wrong.

Interrogation: Apparently only legal if some other country does it.

Interview: The act of having a manager waste your time when applying for a job.

Intimacy: What many relationships lack.

Intimidation: Why most people say and do nothing when something is wrong.

Intolerant: How I feel about the above.

Intoxicating: True love (didn't think I could say something nice in this book, did you)?

Intriguing: The opposite of any modern mystery novel.

Intrusion: What phone calls are during the honeymoon.

Invader: Any relative who shows up unannounced.

Invalid: Any excuse your relative has for showing up unannounced.

Invertebrate: What you are if you don't kick the relative who shows up unannounced out.

Investigation: More often than not, a good way to waste taxpayer money.

Invincible: Anyone appointed to the Supreme Court.

Invisible: Me at a party.

Invitation: What I don't get to a party.

Involuntary: Letting me into a party.

I.O.U.: A form of payment that should be rejected post-haste.

Irish: A group whose population is larger in Boston than in Ireland.

Ironclad: What your alibi had better be if your wife finds underwear that aren't hers in the car.

Irony: If you really don't know how the above-mentioned underwear got there.

Irrational: How your wife is going to act regardless (see above).

Irresponsible: How you're going to look (see above).

Irreversible: The situation thereafter (see above).

Irritable: Me when I wake up in the morning.

Isolation: What you crave if you live in an apartment complex.

Itch: Lots of trouble depending on where it is.

Ivory: The road to extinction for many animals.

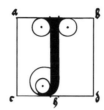

Jabber: What your wife does while the game is on.

Jack: Burned his nuts on a candlestick.

Jackass: See "lobbyist."

Jaded: The attitude with which most people choose to see things.

Jail: Where college students spend the night after having their stomachs pumped for alcohol poisoning.

Jam: That stuff between your toes.

Janitor: The non-politically correct way to say "maintenance engineer."

Japan: That country that kicked our ass with electronics after they lost the war.

Jaw: Something I wish a lot of people I know had wired shut.

Jealous: What you are because you didn't think to write a book like this before I did.

Jelly: The composition of the average spine.

Jellyfish: An individual totally infected with the condition mentioned above.

Jeopardy: What anyone visiting another country is in every time a politician in this country opens his mouth.

Jerk: Indigenous to next door; one is usually found in every neighborhood.

Jesus: One of the most revered figures in history; also the most exploited.

Jig: A trailer park ball.

Job: Where money comes from when you don't borrow it, beg for it, pawn something or sell blood.

Joint: Recreational cigarette, usually found one to a pack of cigarettes or behind the ear.

Jolly: The proper definition is "gay, mirthful, plump and agreeable." I don't know about you, but I don't want to meet this guy.

Journal: A book in which you keep a daily record of lying to yourself.

Journalism: Like the above, but you lie to everyone else.

Journalist: See "village idiot."

Joyful: These kinds of moments are few and far between.

Judge: The guy who barely pays attention when your life is on the line, then either frees or ruins you, depending on how well his day went before you got there (i.e., did he have his coffee, was he laid last night, etc.).

Judgment: What most people pass on you at a glance.

Jug: A lovely thing, usually found in pairs.

Juggernaut: Any *Fortune* 500 company.

Juggle: What the average politician does with the average budget plan.

Jugular: What your ex goes for in divorce court.

Jump: What you are forced to say "how high" to, after divorce court.

Jumper: What you want to be on the roof of the courthouse after divorce court.

Jungle: Your yard when you forget to mow.

Junk: What makes money on eBay while real valuables wash out for pennies on the dollar.

Junta: It means "meeting," but sounds like a naughty word so it's fun to say.

Jury: Something you are randomly forced to participate in against your will, that bores you to death with details you can't understand pertaining to an issue that is none of your business and that you couldn't care less about anyway.

Justice: Hard to find nowadays.

Juvenile: A young person convinced that he is an indestructible, fearless genius; who thinks that he knows everything and isn't scared of you or anybody, and doesn't have to do anything, and can whip your ass--until the slightest little thing happens, and he whimpers and cries for his mommy.

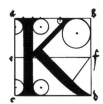

Kaleidoscope: What your glasses become when you are high.

Kangaroo: Giant rat with a pocket that appears much bigger in movies and on TV than it is in real life.

Keepsake: Crap you buy from a catalog.

Keg: The center of attention at any underage party without a chaperone.

Kelp: Probably makes up 50 percent of your burger when you eat out.

Kennel: Doggy motel.

Kerchief: A permanent tissue.

Kernel: The crunchy part of your popcorn.

Key: Comes to life when you are drunk and takes control of your hand and arm so you can't get in the house.

Kidnap: Something that will get you on TV if you don't mind being shot at or manhandled by the FBI (works better in South America).

Kilo: Will get you the same as the above, but no TV time.

Kilt: I won't make fun; the Scottish have been persecuted enough (love the Scots!).

Kind: Something that most people find it hard to be (hell, this book is proof of that).

Kindergarten: A glorified babysitting facility (really, that applies to all public school).

Kindness: Something that it would almost kill the average person to show even just a little of once in a while.

Kiss: Sometimes it can seal your fate.

Kitten: Everyone should run away and become one someday (private joke for Roxxanne).

Kleptomaniac: Your teenager at the mall when you aren't watching.

Knife: Most people have one hanging out of their backs whether they realize it or not.

Knowledge: To those without any, a highly underrated concept.

Label: What we put on people before we know them.

Labor: Takes up more than half our lives.

Laboratory: Where they prove that you *are* the dad.

Laborer: Someone who gets paid pennies for sweat.

Labyrinth: Any community hospital.

Lacerate: To shave with a dull razor.

Lack: An effect of being below middle class.

Lackluster: Most relationships.

Lackey: Gang member.

Lactation: A drink for Dad in the middle of the night without having to leave the bedroom.

Lagoon: Many back yards after rainfall.

Lame: Television sitcoms.

Landlord: A real bastard.

Language: What foreign citizens pretend they can't understand.

Lap: If you are a mall Santa, this is where the kids pee.

Lapse: What most people do after their parole has expired.

Larceny: More an act of jealousy than desperation.

Lascivious: Anyone interested in taking part in the porno industry.

Laugh: What most people are likely to do if you hurt yourself.

Laundry: That mountain behind the bathroom door.

Lavatory: Fancy way of saying "the crapper."

Lavish: What most wealthy people do on themselves instead of helping the less fortunate.

Law: Seems to only apply to the law-abiding.

Lawsuit: You're not American if you haven't been tangled up in one of these.

Lawyer: Professional liar.

Laxative: Human Roto-rooter.

Lay: What the guy next to you in the bar wants.

Lazy: What the rest of the world thinks Americans are.

Lead: What's in the original layer of paint in every old house.

Leadership: Only seems to be taught in the Boy Scouts anymore.

League: Worthless if it's minor.

Leak: Won't stop no matter how tightly you turn the faucet.

Leap year: If you are born on this day, you can stay young longer (on paper).

Lease: A contract designed to make you overpay for a crummy apartment.

Leaseholder: Sucker.

Ledger: Where you hide your assets.

Lecture: To bore people into comas.

Left-handed: An unpopular way to write.

Legacy: Something few people leave behind anymore.

Legality: Something a company squeezes by on in order to screw over its employees.

Legalize: Turning something stupid into a law so you can get away with it.

Legendary: What some of the things that company CEOs have been getting away with recently are.

Legislation: Wastes incredible amounts of time and money.

Legitimate: What few children are anymore.

Legitimize: To administer a DNA test.

Leisure: What I want my life to be.

Lender: Legal loan shark.

Leprosy: What homeless people must have since no one wants to bother with them.

Lethal: A fart on the elevator.

Lethargic: Students in algebra class.

Leucopathy: The extreme opposite of a tan.

Lewd: Most guys in a strip club.

Lexicographer: An incredibly tedious and boring job.

Liability: Something that is terrible to be stuck with.

Liar: Anyone on a witness stand.

Liberal: What political parties like to accuse each other of being.

Liberty: According to lore, you can either have this or death (which is really free is a matter of opinion).

Library: A building coated in dust because not enough people visit there anymore.

Lick: Don't get me started.

Lie: What comes out of a mouth during conversation.

Life: The hardest job you'll ever hate.

Lifeguard: Not as attractive as they look on TV.

Light: Something people are blind to regardless of its abundance.

Light-fingered: Teens at the mall.

Light-footed: Teens running from the mall after being light-fingered.

Lighter: What every teen has in his jacket pocket.

Likeable: You become more of this the more attractive you are.

Lime: The only way certain beers are palatable.

Limited: Human patience.

Limp: What you fake to get a handicapped plate from the DMV.

Linger: What teens do after school.

Link: There's a weak one in every bunch.

Liquor: Makes up about 40 percent of Dad's bodily fluids.

Listless: The result of the above.

Literature: Not really appreciated anymore.

Litter: Glorified sand.

Litter-box: Where the cats piss after they've done it everywhere else in the house.

Livelihood: What you kiss goodbye after divorce court.

Load: What you drop in your pants after you hear the judge's ruling in divorce court.

Loaf: What you turn into at work after divorce court. .

Lobster: An aquatic cockroach that you overpay for in seafood restaurants.

Locate: What you should be doing to your kids when you haven't heard from them by 10:00 p.m. on weekends.

Lock: What you would do with your kids' windows and doors if you did locate them (see above).

Locker: Nerd condominium.

Logic: Doesn't seem to apply to real life anymore.

Loiterer: A teen at an arcade or movie theater.

Lonesome: Too many of us.

Long-winded: Any of your uncle's stories.

Longing: What many do for the girlfriend or boyfriend of someone else.

Loofah: Should be one in every bathtub.

Loophole: The best way out of court.

Lore: Often too indistinguishable from reality.

Lost: Dad on any right turn.

Lottery: Slower than burning your money.

Lovable: Any pet until it grows up.

Love: Fuel for the soul (and like most fuels, we burn it).

Loveless: What most of us truly are.

Lover: What we become content with instead of actual love.

Loyalty: What is lacking that makes us be content with only a lover.

Lubricant: Quite sporting.

Luck: No such thing.

Lucky: What the old lady at the slots thinks she is when she wins $50 after having spent $700.

Luggage: What you use to carry your life with you on vacation.

Lullaby: A song that will make any adult quite insane after heard for the fiftieth consecutive time.

Lunacy: Working as a cashier for more than five years in a row.

Lurdane: Any widow's boyfriend.

Luscious: Me.

Lust: A male condition that helps generate the porno industry.

Lustful: Men on the beach.

Luxury: Something I just can't afford.

Macabre: Popular with the kids.

Macaroni: Popular with the kids, but a better choice than something macabre.

Mace: Popular with joggers.

Machine: What we are in the age of.

Mad: What super fans are.

Madhouse: My house.

Magazine: A picture book of perfume and clothing ads for dizzy teenage girls.

Magic: There's none left in the world.

Magnet: An ornament for the fridge.

Magnificent: My profile.

Mail: Always late unless it's junk.

Majority: Who is supposed to have their say, unless the minority is radical.

Make-believe: The world we all must be living in, not to speak our minds.

Makeup: How a woman buries her face trying to look younger while she makes herself older.

Mall: The beginning of the end for small business.

Malnutrition: A condition that affects too many of our children.

Malpractice: A good way to pick up a settlement.

Man: The undoing of the earth.

Manager: A creepy little person who thinks his title means he is a demigod.

Mannequin: More lifelike than most celebrities.

Manhole: It all depends on your point of view.

Manhood: Something few adult males reach.

Manipulate: To trick an employee into working overtime without the pay.

Manlike: Too many women are this.

Manliness: What too many men think they have.

Manometer: Gaydar.

Mansion: Only affordable if you cut a platinum album.

Manslaughter: Cheating on your husband with another woman.

Manufacturer: A person whose job it is to make your already poor quality products with even cheaper materials.

Manuscript: Often not worth the paper it's printed on.

Map: A paper puzzle that, once opened, is near impossible to close again.

Marble: When older, you tend to lose these.

Margarine: Looks like butter, made from animal fat and/or vegetable oil (you would be surprised how few people know that).

Marine: Sorry kids, no diss for the Marines (*hoo-rah!*).

Marionette: Any politician who accepts large campaign contributions.

Marketable: Just about everything.

Marketing: Keeping track of your bad spending habits so the company can take more advantage of you later.

Marooned: What you are when you miss the last bus.

Marriage: A grave that you yourself dug.

Married: Buried.

Mars: The next planet we are going to screw up.

Masculinity: Often, an illusion.

Mask: Something we create to fool everyone else, while we are really fooling ourselves.

Masochism: A little too much for my taste.

Masquerade: Employees being assembled and asked how much they love the company.

Massacre: Company downsizing.

Master stroke: Premature ejaculation.

Masturbate: Taking pretending to the next level.

Matador: He's either really brave or really stupid.

Materialistic: The new age of man.

Maternity: Currently a state that is unappreciated.

Maturity: Something that is reached physically long before it is reached mentally.

Meddlesome: Older relatives.

Mediator: Someone appointed by the court to make an already sticky situation even more nasty.

Megaphone: Your mother-in-law's mouth.

Membership: Not always what it's cracked up to be.

Menstruation: Now easy to control with harmful drugs.

Mention: What your wife always seems to forget to do about having been shopping.

Merchandise: In today's world, this is worth more than your life.

Messenger: The one who is often shot.

Meter: That thing on the side of the house you wish they would send someone out to read instead of having the computer estimate it all the time.

Migrant: Someone who jumps the border and takes your job (you didn't want it anyway, so quit whining).

Mild: No such thing when it comes to hot sauce.

Millionaire: There's one on every game show (before taxes).

Milestone: Often missed by parents.

Mime: Annoying to the point of near insanity.

Miracle: Often, a fraud.

Mirage: Often a miracle.

Mirror: What many look into but few actually face.

Misalliance: Proposals between countries, in most cases.

Misappropriate: A nice way of saying "rip someone off."

Misbehave: What the kids do when you aren't looking.

Mischief: What the kids are up to the rest of the time.

Misconception: Any notion that you have about the kids being perfect little angels.

Miscount: Taking a vote.

Misdeed: Counting the vote.

Misdemeanor: What it is when you get caught shuffling votes.

Misdirection: Why shuffling votes isn't tried as a felony.

Misemploy: To hire the guy who did the above.

Miserable: What we are as a result of the above.

Misgovernment: Why all of the above goes on.

Misinformed: What we are by the press on the subject of the above.

Misinterpretation: What politicians blame it on when they get caught.

Misjudged: What politicians claim to be.

Misled: What we are as a nation.

Missionary: In many cases, someone who goes to another country ostensibly to help the needy, but really to try to convert people instead. Or, a really boring position (use your imagination on that one).

Mistake: What you make when you forget the condom.

Mistress: Pretty damn expensive.

Mistrust: What having a mistress can create.

Misuse: What most people do with power.

Moan: If she does this, you are doing fine.

Mock: What someone is really doing when they seem like they are being cute.

Mob: Intelligent people who turn stupid when in a group.

Model: A person who is paid for looking good (where's my check?).

Moderation: Something most people do not understand.

Modern: Not all it's cracked up to be.

Modesty: A lost art.

Money: What you live and die for.

Money pit: Your home improvement project.

Monopolize: The goal of any modern company.

Monster: What a modern company becomes in order to reach its goal.

Monthly: How often you have to avoid your wife.

Moo: Your girlfriend's native language.

Moonshine: Another use for corn syrup.

Morality: Something you hear about all the time but rarely see in common practice.

More: It's never enough.

Mortgage: Enough to make you want to hang yourself.

Mortuary: Where you are by the time you get your mortgage paid off.

Motherhood: Not the same as having a baby.

Mourner: What your relatives are, up until they find out you left them out of your will.

Moustache: A clever way to disguise long nose hairs.

Multitasking: Slave labor at its best.

Murder: Remaking old movies.

Muscular: What guys who suck in their guts think they look like.

Music: A matter of opinion.

Musk: They put this in cologne to make men smell good?

Musty: How musk smells to me.

Mutilation: Too much plastic surgery.

Myth: Many legends.

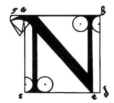

Nag: What most wives asking questions sound like to husbands.

Naive: Most teenage girls are this when they listen to teenage boys.

Nap: Given to children who can't sleep and denied adults who can.

Napkin: What you are supposed to use at meals instead of your sleeve.

Nappy: Untamed hair.

Narrate: To make boredom audible.

Narrow-minded: The political views of potential candidates.

Nasty: Underwear on the third day.

Nationality: Getting more and more confusing every day.

Nature: Unappreciated.

Navigate: Something that is almost impossible to do in the car if there are children present.

Nazi: *Don't* get me started.

Necropolis: Florida.

Needless: About one-third of the national budget.

Nefarious: The true nature of many electoral candidates.

Negligent: What many parents are with their children.

Negotiate: What many detainees are willing to do when they have someone else to blame.

Neighbor: Someone who keeps you up at 2:00 a.m. with loud music and throws trash on your lawn.

Neighborhood: Losing value all the time.

Nerve: Something we swear is about to be struck for the last time every time someone tries to write a check in line ahead of us in the supermarket.

Neurotic: The person writing the check in line ahead of us at the supermarket.

Neuter: Something we do to cats and dogs so we can shirk responsibility for them and let them run wild.

Newspaper: Makes great lining for cat litter boxes.

Nibble: A really irritating way to eat.

Nightcap: Last drink of the night before the next one.

Nightmare: Tax season.

Nincompoop: Your manager.

Nipple: Fun dial.

Nitwit: Your daughter's fiancé.

Nomination: Given to people you never heard of based on their wealth.

Normal: Hard to define anymore.

Nostalgia: Very marketable these days.

Nostril: Practice holes for future bowlers.

Noxious: The odor that comes from the digestion of fast food.

Nuns: The real Untouchables.

Nutcracker: A horse without a saddle, to its rider.

Nutrition: Can't be found in anything on the menu anymore.

Nymphomaniac: The desired personality of a blind date (for him).

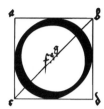

Oaf: Your husband after the first year.

Oasis: Your neighbor's yard in the summer if you don't have a pool and he does.

Oatmeal: Orphanage food.

Obedience: Something that is easier to get from the family dog than your spouse.

Obesity: A common characteristic of American citizens.

Obfuscate: To make campaign promises.

Obituary: The fifteen minutes of fame that Andy Warhol promised.

Object: What most men treat their girlfriends like.

Objection: Something there isn't enough of at weddings.

Object lesson: When all the things that your parents warned you about when you wouldn't listen actually happen to you.

Obligation: Child support.

Obliging: Prostitution.

Obliterate: What we do when we try to "civilize" a third world country.

Oblivious: How most people go through the day.

Obnoxious: Any customer with a complaint.

Observant: State troopers when pulling you over after several other people sped past faster than you.

Obsessed: The state of being an ex-boyfriend.

Obstruction: Something you don't realize that you can go to jail for until it's too late.

Obtainable: The ugly girl.

Obvious: Most lies.

Occupancy: Often exceeded in most apartments.

Odds: Only good if you're the dealer.

Offal: Hotdog stuffing.

Offender: The guy who gets bail before you do.

Offensive: The kid you always have to sit next to in the school cafeteria.

Office: Prison.

Official: Screwing you over with paperwork to back it up.

Offspring: The undesirable and often unwanted carbon copies of the human race.

Ogre: Dad after a few beers.

Ogress: Mom after her vodka.

Oil: A toxic fluid found in the ground that is worth more than your life in most cases.

Oily: The skin of most teenagers.

Old-fashioned: You are this if you speak proper English with no profanity.

Omen: What every extinct species should be taken as.

Omit: What political candidates tend to do with certain aspects of their pasts.

Omnibus: A great way to pass laws that shouldn't be legal.

Omnipotence: The act of becoming the CEO of a multi-billion-dollar company.

Omnipotent: Goes with above.

Omnipresence: Goes with above and a PC.

Omnivorous: Americans.

One-sided: Every story in court.

Onlooker: Every person who watches and does nothing.

Onslaught: The media's reaction when information about a trial leaks out.

Ooze: What little kids' noses do all day.

Openhearted: A rare quality in today's world.

Opera: Rarely appreciated.

Operation: When you pay incredible sums of money to put your life in someone's hands while being subjected to unbearable pain at the same time.

Operator: The person you have to wait forty-five minutes for when you call a 1-800 number.

Opinion: Something everyone is entitled to if they're not too afraid to have one.

Opossum: Likely to end up on the menu depending on how far south you are.

Opportunity: A seldom-noticed, often wasted event.

Oppression: Something you don't notice as much when it happens to others.

Optimism: Setting yourself up for disaster.

Ordinary: The true lives of most people who brag about themselves.

Organic: The polar opposite of the content of most diets.

Organically: The polar opposite of most farming techniques.

Organism: The microscopic example of what you are eating instead.

Organize: Something most people find impossible to do.

Orgasm: Worth its weight in gold.

Orgy: A Hollywood party with no cameras.

Osteopathy: Medically, not good for business.

Ostrich: Where you get the really big drumsticks.

Ounce: What you smoke your life away by.

Ourselves: What we consider to be the most important thing in life.

Outbid: What someone does to piss you off on eBay.

Outbreak: How pimples congregate on young skin.

Outcast: The average teenager in your community.

Outcome: What the average teenager can't foresee when he acts the way he does.

Outfit: What the average teenager is more interested in than his grades.

Outgrow: What the teenager does to those outfits after a couple of months.

Outmaneuver: It used to be possible before police helicopters.

Outpatient: How the hospital tortures you from a distance.

Outsider: What you feel like at a party.

Outstanding: Firefighters (no, really).

Outwit: What you do to poorly educated individuals before they hit you.

Overalls: Baby pants.

Overbearing: Any rules set forth by a parent.

Overburden: Any extra assignment given to you by your boss.

Overcharge: What a convenience store owner does with every item he sells.

Overcoat: Shoplifting attire.

Overcrowd: What you do at a club when you announce ladies' night.

Overdo: Writing a book of sarcastic definitions after having someone say, "damn, you're so sarcastic, you could probably write a book about it" and taking them seriously.

Overdose: Doesn't kill as often as you would think.

Overdue: Most library books.

Overflowing: Not a good way to leave a toilet.

Overhear: Eavesdrop.

Overhung: What most guys pretend to be in the bar.

Over-issued: Internet trial discs.

Overlord: What the title "manager" is often mistaken for.

Overproduction: The folly of most manufacturers.

Overrated: Celebrities by the media.

Overrun: Cashiers during Christmas season.

Overstock: Where anything you're looking for on the shelves in a department store is when the clerk tells you they are out.

Overvalued: Most items in an antique store.

Overweight: A state of being that makes you pay double for charter tickets (i.e., airplane, bus, cross-country train, etc.)

Oyster: An aphrodisiac? Are they serious?

Pacification: Making cable available for utility discounts to welfare recipients.

Pacifier: Disgusting in the mouth of a teenager.

Pacifist: Someone who never had to defend their own life.

Pac-man: Before the video age, this was a man with a backpack.

Paddle: A device for someone who believes in not sparing the rod.

Paganism: Putting money ahead of spirituality.

Pageant: Not meant for children.

Pain: Beauty.

Painful: Life.

Painstaking: Love.

Palatable: Barely, when it comes to frozen dinners.

Palm: Spends more time with your dick than anyone else.

Palmist: Someone who does it for you (see above).

Palm oil: What the palm uses (see above).

Pamper: What the palm does (see above).

Panic: What you do when someone knocks on the bathroom door while you are being "pampered" (see above).

Paper: The outcome of every tree.

Parable: Something most know and few understand.

Parade: Not so much fun when the weather is below zero.

Paradise: The earth before man.

Paraphrase: What human resources cannot do during an interview.

Parasite: Any relative that drops by regularly during dinner.

Parasol: A really gay umbrella.

Parcel: A football for mailmen.

Park: City dump.

Parking garage: Where you pay to have your car broken into.

Parliament: A group of men who try so hard to make witty sarcastic remarks about each other to look clever, that they don't get much else done.

Parole: Half the country is on this.

Partial: When you haven't quite lost all of your teeth.

Participate: What your parents force you to do at school events.

Partnership: What a relationship should be more than.

Passion: Needed in lovemaking to make it any good.

Passionless: Modern art.

Password: Something your computer requires that you can never remember.

Paste: Something kids eat in kindergarten.

Pastry: Should be with every meal.

Paternity: Often determined in court.

Pathetic: The fact that court is where paternity is often determined.

Patient: The worst thing to be in a hospital.

Patriot: A dying breed.

Patriotic: A matter of opinion.

Pawn: Soldier on the battlefield.

Pawnbroker: A person licensed to rip you off.

Peace: What many offer and few deliver.

Peacemaker: The man in the crosshairs.

Pedestal: Where most celebrities, athletes and politicians put themselves.

Penance: Something people only appreciate when it's someone else doing it.

Penetration: The goal of any guy in a nightclub.

Penis: The main focus of almost every male.

Penmanship: A lost art.

Penniless: Most of us, two days after getting our paycheck.

Pension: Not always worth the wait.

Penthouse: Where the action is.

People: The downfall of society.

Perdition: The road of good intentions.

Perform: What your date expects you to do if he paid for dinner.

Perfume: Not a substitute for a bath.

Perjury: Sworn statements most of the time.

Permanent: Most mistakes.

Permission: What your kids do things without.

Peroxide: More fun to watch on a cut than alcohol.

Perpetrate: To be a modern rap performer.

Perplexity: What I am in a state of every time I hear hip-hop nowadays.

Personality: What celebrities lack after they become comfortable with the make-believe ones they show to the public.

Perspiration: Good for the skin; since when did this become a bad thing?

Perspire: Go on, do it, you know you want to.

Pervert: There's one in every family and about ten in every neighborhood.

Pessimism: A lonely way to get through life.

Pest: A child who asks too many damn questions.

Pet: Often treated better than a person.

Petrify: To get Botox treatment.

Pharmacy: Probably getting to be one of the most confusing places to work in America.

Phenomenal: Either how many drugs are on the market, or the fact that they made it there in the first place.

Philanthropist: A lying bastard.

Philosopher: Nowadays, comedians.

Philosophy: Should be taught in high school so college students can actually pass the class when they take it again, or, the art of over explaining the obvious.

Phobia: An excuse for your bad habits and pointless superstitions.

Photograph: Can make you or break you.

Photographer: Someone who's for culture, or a vulture.

Physique: Either chiseled hard or loaded with lard.

Pie: All good girls get some (private joke for Antoinette).

Picket: To leave your job and whine that someone else took it.

Pickpocket: Someone who gets paid for groping on the subway.

Picnic: Not likely to be an enjoyable experience in most inner city parks.

Piercing: Depending on where it is, often a desperate cry for attention.

Pig: What your boyfriend is when he's not a dog.

Pigeon: Flying rat.

Pillage: To open a major department store in a small Midwestern town.

Pillager: The CEO of above.

Pimp: A person with low self esteem who takes advantage of someone else's even lower self esteem.

Pimple: A good way to end a date before it starts.

Pinch: A good way to get smacked.

Pine: A sacrificial tree that is decapitated and offered up for Christmas.

Pineapple: Not quite an apple, nor does it grow on a pine.

Piracy: How you get all those crappy, scratchy bootleg copies of CDs and DVDs.

Piss: Food coloring for snow.

Pistol: Should be one under every pillow.

Pizza: Food of the gods; I could live off of this stuff forever (one cool point to the Italians).

Placenta: Seems natural enough until you see the cat eat it.

Plagiarism: Setting yourself up for disaster.

Plagiarist: Evil son of a bitch.

Plaintiff: Another evil son of a bitch.

Plaque: What the company gives you when they don't want to compensate you for something.

Plastic: Eventually, everything.

Platinum: The new gold.

Player: Usually a bum with a lot of talk.

Plaything: What advertisers want us to think a new car is.

Pleading: The last resort a guy may use to get sex.

Pleasurable: Can be quite expensive, depending on the circumstances.

Pleasure: An industry all on its own.

Plentiful: Apparently it gives you the right to waste.

Pleonasm: Answering questions in a political forum.

Plunger: A tool that seems to always be there except when you have a clog.

Plutocrat: The kind of person who makes large campaign contributions.

Poem: Nowadays, any scribble.

Pointless: Trying to explain anything logical to people.

Poison: Most new movies to the box office.

Police: Some are squeaky clean, some are dirty and mean.

Polite: Something anyone in a department or grocery store should be paid extra to be.

Politically Correct: Being forced to lie to yourself.

Politician: Some are honest and just, some you should definitely mistrust.

Polka: Why people think you are a freak if you're from Pittsburgh.

Pollution: Our reward for industry.

Polyandry: Something I think that few women dream of.

Polygamist: Something every guy dreams of being.

Polygraph: How you bust your husband on TV talk shows.

Pompous: A requirement for rappers.

Pornography: That collection of unmarked VCR tapes in the box under your husband's side of the bed.

Porn star: Someone who has convinced herself that degrading herself will make her famous in a productive way.

Position: The only thing a porn star may ever be famous for.

Possession: It's everything in the eyes of the law.

Possessive: Most young men in a relationship.

Possible: Almost anything.

Postage: Bound to increase.

Postal: A term that now brings to mind temporary insanity because of one or two isolated incidences (give them a break, huh?).

Postman: A guy with skinny legs who wears shorts and a pith helmet without feeling goofy.

Postmortem: What most people are by the time you decide to reconcile with them.

Post office: Where you will spend half your life in line.

Potent: Cough syrup.

Potential: What few ever reach.

Potluck: Always means you'll find green bean casserole or Bundt cake.

Poultry: Fatty meat garnished with penicillin and steroids.

Poverty: Not always the fault of the establishment.

Powerless: How you feel about poverty, regardless of whose fault it is.

Praise: Something children need more of rather than chastising.

Prank: Not as funny as you think.

Prayer: All too often, when someone grovels to God for something they don't really need or deserve.

Preacher: Not always as accurate with the Word as he thinks.

Precious: What the Word is, and why it should not be altered or misinterpreted.

Precognition: When Mom accuses you of things you are about to do when you go out.

Predestination: Not practical at all.

Prefabricate: What you do before the trial.

Pregnancy: One of the most beautiful and, sadly, also one of the most despised aspects of being female.

Pregnant: A state of being for a female that can be one of the most blessed events in her life if she's smart enough to understand it before it's over.

Prejudice: Using ignorance to fuel ignorance.

Preoccupied: What too many parents are when their children need them the most.

Prescription: A license to chemically lobotomize.

Preserve: Where poachers hang out.

President: An office that once upon a time held the utmost respect, when respectable men held the office.

Press: A group that will get to the bottom of anything even if they have to dig the hole themselves, no matter who is buried in the process.

Pressure: What the press puts on all the wrong people.

Prestige: What the press had once upon a time.

Pretender: Anyone with an outlandish story about himself.

Preventive: Almost every disaster in life if someone cares to get involved.

Prey: What consumers are to advertisers.

Price: All the consumers seem to care about.

Priceless: The things we overlook when we replace morals with materialism.

Prick: Your mom's new boyfriend.

Pride: What your mom seems to have lost to be dating her new boyfriend in the first place.

Primal: A part of us we all try to suppress unless we are lucky enough to be boxers or football players.

Primeval: What any third world country looks like until you walk a mile in the residents' shoes.

Primitive: Community healthcare.

Princess: The kind of girl I can do without.

Principal: In my experience, the chief bullshit artist at a public school.

Printer: A device that is out of date by the time you get it out of the box.

Priority: Always seems to be out of order.

Prison: Where half the fathers in this country are.

Prisoner: That guy Mom visits twice a week in the morning.

Privacy: Something they say we are all entitled to but still have to pay for.

Privilege: Something you used to get for having skill but now get by kissing ass or being wealthy.

Prizefight: A profession where you are guaranteed to make enough money to pay for the brain damage you receive on the job (hopefully).

Probation: Better than jail if you can pass the occasional urine test.

Probe: The last thing you want to see your doctor with.

Problem: Something everyone sees when it belongs to someone else.

Prodigy: The overlooked child.

Produce: An edible substance grown by overworked, underpaid and unappreciated farmers and found in supermarkets that provides you with your RDA of pesticides and steroids. .

Products: More important than the workers who make them.

Profanity: A type of language you learn from public school or your parents.

Professional: What everyone claims to be when they are trying to justify their immoral behavior.

Profit: The modern equivalent of thirty pieces of silver.

Prognosis: Makes a condition worse by eliminating hope.

Prohibition: Worked better than you think if you read the history.

Project: A miserable place to live that is somehow supposed to be cool if you are from there.

Promise: Something humans should never do since they almost never keep them.

Promotion: A reward you give to the biggest ass-kisser.

Pronunciation: Something schools must not teach anymore, since I can't decipher what most young people are saying.

Propaganda: Anything you hear around election time.

Property: Worth getting shot for.

Propose: To set yourself up for the kill.

Prosperity: It's everyone's right, but there are no guarantees.

Prostitute: Nothing for money and the dicks for free, (must be a prostitute to get this one).

Protection: What the prostitute needs to get out of the profession.

Proud: What most people should be but are not.

Provide: What parents should do more than.

Provoke: What bullies do to get you into trouble.

Psalm: Something that is memorized more than it is understood.

Psychic: Someone who scams you out of money with psycho/social analysis twisted into whatever you think you need to hear.

Psychological: What most ailments truly are.

Psychologist: Someone paid to pretend to care.

Psychology: A science that tells you what you think based on averages, without keeping in mind that all minds are unique.

Puberty: The beginning of the end.

Public: Anything that is supposed to be for everyone even though it's city or government property.

Publicity: A bonus or a curse, depending on what you've been up to.

Pullover: Not a good thing to hear while you're driving.

Pulp: Any food after you give it to the baby, whether he eats it or not.

Pulse: Stops for a second when your prom date steps down the stairs for the first time (ideally).

Pump: What you use on your dick (not mine, *yours*).

Pumpkin: The most wasted and trivialized of all vegetables.

Punch: Where you dump the vodka.

Punctuality: A lack of this is the reason most people have trouble finding work.

Punishment: Would probably be more fair if we did it ourselves.

Pupil: A young person asleep at a desk.

Puppet: Whoever takes the blame when a company gets busted for fraud or illegal dumping.

Puppy: Really cute until you try to train the damn thing not to crap on your carpets.

Purchasable: Zoning permits and state construction contracts.

Pure: Nothing anymore except bottled water.

Purify: What we have to do to everything, even the water.

Pussy: A fluffy little kitty (awww).

Pustule: What you never want to see on your pussy.

Putrefaction: What you never want to smell from your pussy.

Pyrotechnic: A fancy word for blowing shit up.

Python: A really cool pet up until it closes in on fifty pounds.

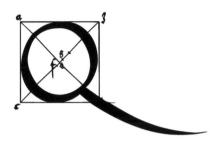

Quack: HMO-approved doctor.

Quagmire: Cheap land in Florida.

Quaker: A human spectacle for the amusement of tourists in Pennsylvania.

Qualification: Something most jobs require more of than they are willing to pay for.

Quality: More likely to be found in products made overseas as opposed to products made at home.

Quantity: Buying in this is the only way to get a half-decent price.

Quarantine: What most people should be in during the winter months.

Quartermaster: Cool-sounding job title.

Queen: My next wife.

Question: Often something rather stupid.

Questionable: Most business practices.

Questionnaire: Comes after the initial job application (designed to use up two or more hours of your time).

Quickly: The opposite of how any express line at the supermarket moves.

Quietly: The opposite of how any child plays.

Quintuple: A hard birth.

Quiz: How the professor brings down the grade average.

Quote: Something that someone who is more clever than you are said.

Rabbit: The only animal that makes it across the road without being a pancake.

Rabble: Crowds in front of concerts.

Rabid: Crowds in front of concerts.

Race: A card not used when needed, or thrown down when it isn't.

Racial: Not a good enough excuse to hate.

Racist: A person with too much free time and no constructive way to use it.

Radar: Women have this when you are late coming home from work.

Radiation: Emits from your smoke detector (really).

Radical: Takes everything too seriously.

Radio: Would have been extinct if not for cars.

Raffle: What a church calls gambling so as not to get into trouble.

Ragamuffin: What your kids go to school looking like if you let them dress themselves.

Rage: What you feel when the boss tells you what to do, and you know he's wrong, but he won't listen.

Rain: What people beg for when there isn't any but whine about when there is.

Raise: Smaller than you had hoped.

Raisin: Grandma.

Rancid: The fridge with too many leftovers.

Random: Bullets meant for someone else.

Ransack: What you do to the house while looking for the keys that are in your coat pocket.

Ransom: Paying off a layaway.

Rap: Crap.

Rape: The act of proving what an incredible loser you are.

Rare: What everyone claims their item is on eBay.

Rat: The one the cops let go.

Rationally: How most people don't think.

Rattlesnake: Telemarketer.

Rave: Used to mean "delirium," but now it's a party.

Ravenous: Kids who skip school lunch (but can you blame them)?

Raw: Lips in winter.

Razor: A device for nicking the face.

Reaction: Seems to be slower while driving.

Realistic: Something that it is hard for many people to be.

Reasonable: Something that it is hard for many people to be.

Rebate: Making you wait for your discount.

Rebel: What every young girl is looking for in a boyfriend until she gets stuck with one.

Rebound: How most guys get their second girlfriend.

Recede: What your hair does to get away from your ugly face and bad breath.

Receipt: What most people don't think they need until they do need it and can't find it.

Receptionist: A secretary who had *better not* be better looking than your wife, if you know what's good for you.

Recession: What seems to happen with each new election.

Recklessly: How people drive when they borrow your car.

Recollection: Something most people are not capable of after a few drinks.

Recommendation: The least a company can offer you after you lose your job.

Reconsider: What most people do when it's too late.

Record: What I should do to every phone conversation.

Recover: Hard to do after a long relationship.

Rectify: Often impossible.

Red-handed: The worst way to get caught.

Redress: Something you seem to have to do after almost every diaper change.

Red tape: What we get tangled up with every time we try to get anything done in court or with business.

Redundant: Newspaper articles.

Re-elect: Punish your community all over again.

Re-enact: How they make money in the South.

Re-engage: Punishing yourself all over again.

Referee: The guy who interrupts the action so often you could hang him.

Refinery: A factory where the main function seems to be killing fish.

Reflection: What you should take a good hard look at before you go any further with your life.

Reform: What you are supposed to do in prison.

Refrigeration: Having no heat in the winter.

Refugee: One who comes to America by the boatload.

Register: A machine operated by a cashier that never has correct change (not that the cashier can count it anyway).

Regret: What we have when it's too late.

Rehearsal: When something sounds really good; then we say it in public.

Reimburse: A word that relatives don't understand when you lend them money.

Reinvestment: Wasting your money twice.

Reissue: Making money off of the same idea twice.

Rejection: Something you should get used to if you are into the bar scene.

Relapse: What many parolees would do if they didn't have U.A.'s, (a Urinary Analysis to you honest citizens).

Relationship: Not all it's cracked up to be.

Relative: An annoying person we are often forced to deal with.

Relaxation: Something we cannot achieve with children in the house.

Relentless: A woman in an argument.

Relief: Getting to the toilet after a five-hour drive.

Religion: Not the same as faith or devotion.

Reluctant: What we are to job duties.

Remark: Something made behind your back.

Remarry: To self-destruct.

Remorse: Often only shown in appearance.

Rendezvous: Sneaking around on the wife.

Renounce: What your parents end up doing when they reach their limit.

Rent: Never on time.

Rental: Not worth the rent.

Renter: A person who has better things to do with their money.

Repair: What the landlord thinks a few coats of paint will do to a dilapidated apartment.

Repay: What the landlord is not likely to do with your deposit.

Repellant: Something that seems to attract mosquitoes (since they are attracted to body heat and not odor).

Repetition: The function of most jobs.

Replication: Most antiques.

Reporter: Someone who is paid to read from a teleprompter.

Represent: What your children do to your character (so raise them right).

Reproachable: Most musical performers.

Republican: God knows anymore.

Repulsive: Cosmetics.

Reputation: Generally not as good as people say theirs are.

Request: Something that is denied if it will cost someone anything.

Rescue: What you do to yourself when you find a better job.

Reservation: Overpaying for dinner.

Resignation: A polite way to tell your boss to stick it.

Resist: What we do when we are fired even though we bitch and complain about the job every day.

Respect: Something we cannot give to anyone else if we have none for ourselves.

Responsibility: Something we should try taking once in a while instead of blaming everyone else.

Restaurant: Where we eat when we are too lazy to cook.

Restless: Anyone at 4.45 p.m. Monday through Friday.

Resurrection: Viagra induced reaction.

Retail: Where most of the money goes.

Retired: A door greeter in a department store.

Retract: What you do when your words get you into trouble.

Revenge: Wish it were legal.

Reverse: What you do too quickly in order to shred your transmission.

Revival: When you spend seven hours in church.

Revolution: Alternative voting.

Reward: Securing honesty.

Riddle: Any legal document.

Ridiculous: Any legal document.

Righteousness: What you think you have when you don't.

Rim: Recently, associated with a job (use your imagination).

Riot: Generally follows winning a championship.

Risky: Being for the other team during a championship.

Robbery: Inner city land prices.

Robot: What replaced your job.

Rodent: One of a family of animals found in your attic and basement.

Rolling pin: Comes upside your head if you come home in the wrong underwear.

Romance: Dead.

Rope: When someone is doing you wrong, you give him just enough.

Rotary: A way to confuse drivers.

Rover: A lame thing to name your dog.

Royalty: A group of people who think they are better than everyone while showing that they are not.

Rubber: Something you never seem to have when you need it.

Rude: How most slang sounds.

Russian: A people Americans were afraid would invade them with soldiers, who eventually ended up doing it with passports instead.

Sabotage: When one of your coworkers goes drinking with the boss.

Sacred: Few things anymore.

Sacrificial: Employees during company downsizing.

Sad: The state of the world today.

Sadism: When the management makes you multitask without compensation.

Sag: What Grandma's boobs do.

Sailor: Thought of as masculine before the 1970s.

Saint: A fictional character in today's society.

Salad: What vegetarians get stuck with when eating out.

Salary: Often a method of payment that demands so many overtime hours that you wind up making the equivalent of $1.85 per hour.

Salesman: A really annoying bastard.

Saliva: Baby lube.

Salivation: Baby hobby.

Salmon: A fish that is either really determined or really stupid.

Saltpeter: Prison seasoning.

Salvage: Licensed garbage picking.

Salvation: Something that you had better be very careful of if promised by man.

Sample: Free food at the market.

Sampler: Not free.

Sandal: Air-conditioned shoe.

Sanitary: A condition you will *not* find in a public restroom.

Sanity: Can be lost while teaching a high school English class.

Sap: A person who believes that when the sign in the supermarket says "10 for 10," you actually have to buy ten of them to get the sale price.

Sarcastic: This book.

Satan: The entity that everyone likes to blame when they do something stupid or nasty instead of owning up for their own behavior and actions.

Satellite: The beginning of littering the rest of the solar system now that we're almost done with Earth.

Satin: Really nice for bed sheets.

Satire: This book.

Satisfaction: What I get a little of for writing this book.

Saturn: The ball behind Uranus.

Scab: Irresistible to young children.

Scalp: Easier to see, the older you get.

Scaly: Some scalps.

Scandal: Most stories about celebrities that would be no big deal if it were anyone else.

Scarecrow: Absolutely useless.

Scavenger: A kid on Halloween.

Scent: Unfortunately, the best way to identify some people.

Scholarship: The next best thing to mooching off of your parents.

School: An institution devoted to boring children half to death in an effort to prepare them for boring adult lives.

Science: The art of finding ways to fuck everything up.

Scorch: To present a political commentary.

Scotland: One of the most abused nations on Earth with some of the deepest heritage.

Scoutmaster: A grown man dressed like a little kid.

Screamer: The kid you can't wait to drop off at daycare.

Script: Comes with each reality show.

Searchable: Apparently, everybody, under the Patriot Act.

Secluded: Starting to look like a better way to live.

Secret: Easy to give, hard to keep.

Secretary: That woman your wife is suspicious of.

Security: Lots of cameras that no one is watching.

Security guard: Old, unarmed man with a limp.

Sedate: Give someone cough syrup.

Seductive: Any woman who is not your wife.

Seed: Often bad.

Segregate: Set yourself up for disaster.

Seize: What the cops do to your stuff when you get pulled over.

Seizure: What you are likely to have at the arraignment.

Self-confidence: What most people have up until it's actually time to take action.

Self-control: Seriously lacking in today's youth.

Self-educated: These people are often more intelligent than honor students.

Self-esteem: A very neglected human commodity.

Selfish: A very exploited human commodity.

Self-respect: The average person lacks this, which is why he can't respect anything.

Self-righteous: Everyone else.

Self-sufficient: What you think every woman is until you marry her.

Semen: Not sailors.

Senator: Someone you vote for and never see again.

Seniority: Why all those older guys who do nothing still work for the company even though you could do their job more efficiently.

Sensationalism: Tabloids.

Senseless: Tabloids.

Sensitive: The people the tabloids write about.

Sensual: Me in the tub.

Septic: When you are too far away from civilization for a water line.

Sequel: Ruins the memory of a good movie.

Serenity: A noble quest, but near impossible to obtain.

Series: Dragging a bad show out as far as you can.

Servant: Anyone making less than eight dollars an hour.

Servile: The model employee.

Servitude: The life your company wants you to live.

Settle: What most people do in the above situation.

Sex: My favorite pastime.

Sexuality: What guys pretend to have.

Shabbily: How guys do it, (sex that is).

Shaky: How guys are the first time they do it, (still talking sex here).

Shallow: How most guys are after they do it, (ok, last sex pun).

Sham: When guys tell you they love you after you do it, (ok, I lied; this is the last one from above).

Shameless: What it truly is when the above happens.

Shanty: Where men who look for women on the Internet live.

Shapeless: How men who look for women on the Internet look.

Sheep: What the above-mentioned men would go for if they didn't have Internet porn.

Shellshock: The effect on the woman who meets the above-mentioned guy for the first time.

Sheriff: Who the woman mentioned above calls next.

Shin: Where the guy the woman above just met gets kicked while she's making the call to the sheriff.

Shiner: What happens to the above-mentioned guy's eye after the shin incident.

Shipmaster: Really gay-sounding job.

Shipmate: The shipmaster's little friend.

Shipshape: What the shipmaster and his shipmate probably call it when they get together.

Shipwreck: When the above relationship doesn't work out.

Shoplifting: Spontaneous credit.

Snowman: Sounds like a nickname for a really creepy dope dealer.

Shrapnel: What dope dealers should be loaded with.

Shrink: What people would think you needed for saying such a thing as the above comment.

Shrinkage: An excuse men use for having small dicks.

Shrivel: A better explanation for above.

Shrubbery: Some pubic hair.

Shrunken: A better description of above.

Sick room: The bedroom after above.

Sidesaddle: How you don't have to ride if you have any of the above problems.

Signature: Can get you into a lot of trouble depending on where you left it.

Silence: What I could die for when trying to get some sleep.

Silicone: Found in about 40 percent of the breasts in America.

Silly: What the above can be.

Silverware: Actually has to be made from *silver* to be called this, people! Anything else is "flatware" or "utensils"! *Get it right!*

Simian: What some guys act like around a large-chested woman.

Simpleton: What the rest of the guys act like around a large-chested woman.

Simulation: What boobs that big really are.

Sin: The reason why some women get bigger boobs.

Sincere: The rest of the women who get bigger boobs.

Single: A person who thinks he or she is either too good for someone or not good enough.

Sister: That person related to you who steals all of your good clothes and talks to your boyfriend behind your back.

Skeleton: One in every closet.

Skid: You're in trouble if one of these is in your boxers.

Skin: Sensual.

Slack: The natural response of employees to the boss leaving for lunch or vacation.

Slam: What the boss does to slacking employees when he gets back.

Slang: How you talk when you want people to think you're an idiot.

Slave: Me on the job.

Slavedrivers: How I view management.

Slavery: Me being hired for a job.

Slave trade: Minimum-wage jobs.

Sleazy: The kind of women Dad gets involved with after the divorce.

Sleep: Getting to be a priceless commodity.

Sleepless: The reason sleep is priceless.

Sleeveless: Seems like this type of shirt is worn by any guy without the muscle to back it up.

Slippery: Fun, depending on the situation.

Slobber: Not so fun.

Slogan: Adding some stupid words to an asinine product.

Sluggard: Mom's new boyfriend after the divorce.

Slut: Mom after a divorce.

Smack: What I'll probably get from Mom for saying that.

Smoker: A person who is committing suicide, nice and slow.

Smoking: Paying for it while you kill yourself.

Smut: What Dad is really looking for on the Internet.

Snatch: What Dad is looking at pictures of on the Internet.

Snivel: How your coworker got the promotion.

Snow: One of the few things that makes the world look clean anymore.

Snowplow: A huge truck that tears up benches, garbage cans and street signs, and buries them in big snow piles.

Soap: Kids would swear less if we still used this.

Sober: A rare condition for Dad.

Sock: What washers eat.

Sodomy: Unwanted by the army but popular in prison.

Soldier: A profession that used to be much harder before they made boot camp easier.

Son: In many countries, this is more valuable than a daughter.

Soprano: The guy who got the sodomy.

Sorcerer: Many women must be one, I think.

Sorry: My relationships to this point (damn sorcerers).

Soul: An extremely valuable possession that is mistreated by its owner.

Soup: Food for the toothless and the drunks.

Southerner: Someone who "thanks them city folk don't know nuthin'."

Spanish: The native language of the inhabitants of most of the West Coast, although they may or may not be U.S. citizens and likely speak English better than you.

Spanking: Fun when done in moderation.

Spark: A certain something that you think you see in someone that makes her special, without keeping in mind that sparks usually cause fires and burn things down.

Special: Me, naturally.

Specialist: Someone who is overpaid.

Specimen: Us to any drug company.

Spectacular: What advertisers want us to think everything they put on the market is.

Speculation: How we should be thinking about the above.

Speechless: What we would be if we realized how bad some of the above-mentioned stuff really is.

Sperm: Skin cream (I know, that one was pretty bad).

Spew: Army chow.

Spice: The only thing that makes Army chow palatable.

Spine: Something of yours that the boss tries to break when he doesn't have one himself.

Spiritualism: Often, a hoax.

Splendid: Hopefully, this book.

Spoiled: Why your kid doesn't listen to you.

Spokesman: A person who translates someone else's bullshit to the public.

Spontaneous: The best kind of love (see, I can say nice things sometimes).

Sport: Something people watch more of than participate in.

Spouse: The evil twin.

Spread-eagle: How most girls who go out for a modeling job end up.

Spree: What the wife has if she gets your wallet.

Spurt: What happens when you squeeze zits.

Spy: Only cool in the movies.

Squander: What many do with their fortunes after winning the lottery.

Squashed: What happens to lottery-winners' dreams after they win.

Squat: How girls pee in the woods.

Squeal: What girls do when animals creep out of the bushes while they're squatting.

Squeamish: Why the above-mentioned girls squeal.

Squirrel: What the above-mentioned animal usually turns out to have been.

Stab: What the above-mentioned girl would like to do to you for laughing.

Stagger: How you got home from the club after the bouncer took your keys.

Stagnation: Working in a cubicle.

Stalker: Every girl has one, usually an ex.

Stamina: Something guys brag about.

Stampede: What guys in the club do when the good-looking girl walks in.

Standard: Me; I have decided that I am the standard.

Star: What anyone who ever had a walk-on part in any crappy TV show thinks he or she is.

Starvation: Model training.

Statistic: There's one for every damn thing these days.

Stepfather: More of these than original fathers.

Steppingstone: The original father.

Sticker: A cheap reward usually given to children.

Stiff: Your blind date when he notices your cleavage from across the table.

Stimulating: Obviously, your cleavage to your blind date (see above).

Stimulation: What your blind date is probably doing now (see above).

Stockbroker: Someone who buys and sells stock for someone else because he's too smart to risk his own money.

Stock exchange: Three-ring circus.

Stockholder: Either really lucky or really stupid.

Storage: Where your stuff ends up after the fight.

Stowaway: Harder to do on a plane than a boat.

Straddle: What she does when she's on top.

Straggle: What she does when she's tired.

Strange: What people must think I am for saying the above.

Stranger: Someone you should avoid.

Strangler: What the stranger might be, which is why you should stay away from them.

Stray: Any and every animal your kid tries to bring home.

Streaks: The marks in little kids' underwear.

Strip: To take it off.

Stripper: A person who gets paid for taking it off.

Stroke: What you might get a few of from the above-mentioned stripper in certain clubs.

Stubble: You're in trouble if the above-mentioned stripper has some of this.

Stuck-up: What you say the above-mentioned stripper is if she doesn't do some stupid, nasty thing that you asked for.

Stud: What guys in a strip club think they are, which doesn't explain why they are hanging around in a strip club.

Stunning: How the girls look in a strip club (in the dark).

Stupid: What guys are for wasting their time in places like a strip club.

Suave: Me in a suit.

Sublet: Getting screwed on the rent second hand.

Subscription: How you get an overpriced, crappy magazine that you never read.

Subsidy: How you pay for someone else to have an apartment.

Subspecies: What is thought of the people who live this way (see above).

Substitute: The teacher you ignore (even more than the original one).

Subversive: What having a liquor store, a smoke shop and a porno shop in the same place is to the neighborhood.

Subway: The physical personification of "hurry up and wait."

Succulent: What Thanksgiving dinner is before you actually taste it.

Suck: What you think of the Thanksgiving meal after.

Sucker: In many cases, a person who believes the words "I love you".

Suckle: Foreplay.

Suffer: To endure a relationship.

Suffocate: To endure a relationship.

Sugar: A gift from God (see chocolate).

Suggest: The best way to annoy someone.

Suicide: The pussy's way out.

Sunburn: An excuse to "accidentally" slap someone on the back.

Superabundance: What you find in a department store stockroom.

Superficial: What dating is.

Superfine: Me on a date.

Superhuman: Still me.

Superintendent: Glorified janitor.

Supernatural: Me again.

Superstition: Providing an excuse for your stupid habits.

Supervise: To do nothing and get paid for it.

Supervisor: Someone you talk about behind his back.

Support: A judge's order.

Survive: What you can barely do after the above-mentioned order.

Suspicion: A clue that it's time to bail on the relationship.

Swagger: A way you walk that makes you look stupid to everyone but you.

Swallow: She says she can't, but it's a lie.

Swap: When the couple next door asks you to do this, it's time to get some new friends.

Swear: A type of word used all too often in the English language.

Sweepstakes: Something I never win.

Sweetmeat: Obviously, my penis.

Swelling: How my penis got so sweet.

Swindle: What a business that sells rental furniture does.

Swish: What kids in the schoolyard say before the ball bounces off of the rim.

Sybarite: A profession I am entertaining the idea of for the future.

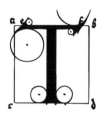

Table: Where families used to eat dinner.

Taboo: Most of my preferences.

Tack: Goes on the seat in front of you in grammar school.

Tackle: Happens to you if you are unpopular, whether you have the ball or not.

Tact: What few people have when giving advice.

Tactics: What people use when setting you up on a blind date.

Tag: A child's game that gives them an excuse to slap each other. Or, an adolescent's game to give them an excuse to feel each other up.

Tailor: Someone who doesn't get much business anymore.

Take: What most do instead of give.

Talent: What few television actors possess.

Talented: Lap dancers.

Talkative: The kind of person you should avoid in prison.

Talk-show host: Often, a professional Hollywood brownie-scout.

Tally-ho: What fox hunters say to sound gay.

Tambourine: An instrument you play to look gay.

Tamper: What computer networkers do when they are fired.

Tampion: A plug for a cannon (just thought you might want to know where the word "tampon" came from).

Tampon: Something women get men to buy for them to embarrass the men in the supermarket.

Tangle: Fishing line.

Tantalizing: A stripper in a birthday cake.

Tantrum: How children manipulate their parents in public.

Tape: A spool of sticky transparent material that shreds off in little strips with increasing frequency the more you need it.

Tarantula: Really cool; I wish I had one.

Tardy: What I was just about every day in high school.

Target: Any smart kid in a public school.

Taskmaster: A productivity manager.

Tasteless: Boxed pastries.

Tattler: Younger brother or sister.

Tattoo: Better like it, 'cause you're stuck.

Tax: How you are charged for working.

Taxable: Just about everything.

Taxi: A service you pay to take the long way home.

Taxidermy: One of those professions where you sit back and wonder how the hell someone got into that in the first place.

Tea: Better than coffee.

Teacher: Some are underpaid and the rest are overrated.

Team: What the boss tries to convince you that you are part of in order to exploit you. Or, there may be no "I" in it, but there is no "U" in it either!

Tease: A girl stuffed into an outfit that is three sizes too small.

Teat: Goes in your mouth.

Technology: Fast becoming more important than the people who invent it.

Tedious: Life in general.

Teething: A process that allows infants and toddlers to get away with screaming and screaming and screaming.

Telepathy: How I knew that you would buy this book.

Telephone: One of the most annoying inventions in history.

Television: The other most annoying invention in history.

Temper: What the above two items can cause me to lose.

Temptation: Having a woman tell you she doesn't care that you're married.

Temptress: Your wife's sister, if you live in a trailer park.

Tenfold: How much trouble the above sort of thing can get you into.

Tennis: One of the few sports where people keep their mouths shut.

Tenure: Why you can't fire some of those older folks even when they stop being productive.

Terminal: People who lie about themselves.

Terrestrial: Someone who is stuck here.

Terrible: When a guest appears on more than one talk show and says the exact same things the exact same way, over and over and over.

Terrify: To some people, to show the results of a pregnancy test.

Territory: Something that dogs understand better than people.

Terrorism: Taking your anger out on people who don't know what your problem is, and probably aren't responsible for it either.

Test: To set someone up to fail.

Testicle: A lot easier on her without the excess hair.

Textbook: A book you buy for college that costs way too damn much, that you sell back for pennies on the dollar so they can burn someone's wallet with it again.

Texture: Something they add to condoms to try to make them interesting.

Thankless: Often, how people act when you give them something.

Thanksgiving: A historically inaccurate holiday that is the prelude to shopping riots.

Theanthropism: What many evangelists will have you believe they are (watch out).

Therapeutic: I think it was what a good night's rest is (it's been so long I can't remember).

Thermal: The kind of underwear you wish you had when it starts to get really cold.

Thermometer: There are four places you can stick one, and one of them just isn't right.

Thesis: A real pain in the ass.

Thick: A real fine ass.

Thickheaded: The professor who put the thesis on the syllabus.

Thickness: A swelling in the jeans.

Thinking: A function of the brain that is turned off when the thickness comes over you.

Thong: Butt floss.

Throne: Where you are likely sitting while reading this book.

Throwback: Something too many people are starting to resemble.

Thunder: A natural occurrence designed to frighten children.

Thunderbolt: A natural occurrence designed to set off car alarms.

Tigress: What a woman should be in the bedroom.

Time: Something you have too much of when you have nothing to do, and not enough of when you're busy.

Tinfoil: A thin metal sheet that comes on a roll that you crumble into a ball and throw in the microwave for entertainment.

Tinkle: What little kids do to wet the bed.

Tipsy: The girl who came home with you.

Tissue paper: A nice word for the wiping stuff.

Title: A dangerous thing to give to some people (can cause them to get swollen heads).

Tobacco: Nasty stuff and you all know it.

Toilet: A device frivolously used to pollute the ocean. Or, where you are sitting while reading this book.

Tolerate: What our new politically correct society forces us to do with every stupid little thing that other people do.

Tongue: A rather fun tool provided with the human body.

Tonight: When I would like to see the tongue used.

Top-heavy: Eye-catching.

Torture: Just watching the above sometimes.

Totalitarianism: Sometimes I wonder…

Tough: Thanksgiving turkey when you let Grandma help in the kitchen.

Tough Luck: What most pot-luck dinners should be called.

Tourist: A sucker.

Toupee: An item worn by a man fooling himself.

Town council: A group of blithering idiots.

Town hall: Where the above idiots blither.

Townspeople: Who the above idiots blither to.

Toxic: I swear, half the food we eat.

Toy store: Just loads of fun.

Tradition: Not always a good thing.

Tragedy: Television sitcoms.

Trance: What I lapse into during a college lecture.

Transcend: What I intend to do with my life (you should too).

Transparent: Most lies.

Transportation: Should be free.

Trap: A wedding.

Trashy: What the groom's father thinks the bride is.

Traumatic: What the groom's mother thinks the wedding is.

Travesty: What the wedding will turn into if the above keeps up.

Trawl: What they should eat out of at the kiddy table.

Treacherous: Your new mother-in-law.

Treadmill: What the bride is going to need after a few weeks of marriage.

Treasure trove: What the bride sees when she looks at you.

Trespass: A good way to get shot.

Trespasser: Target practice.

Triangle: Not the type of relationship you want to get caught up in.

Tribulation: What is to follow from the above-mentioned triangle.

Tricycle: A lot easier than a bike.

Trilogy: A popular concept in movies recently.

Troglodyte: A teenager who spends all of his time standing around on the corner.

Trojan: Used to be the dweller of an ancient city; now it's a rubber.

Trophy: A hunk of plastic some people would kill for.

Trophy wife: A really dumb but attractive woman.

Troublesome: What a trophy wife is.

True love: Usually not associated with the trophy wife.

Truffle: An edible fungus that people make chocolates with (how did they get these two together?).

Trust: Harder to find, the older you get.

Truth: Even harder to find than trust.

Tug-of-war: Child custody fight.

Turmoil: What the above is for the child.

Turncoat: What the above-mentioned child is when he or she takes advantage of it.

Turning point: When you bust the child doing it (see above).

Turntable: An ancient device used by primitives that resembles the modern CD player.

Tusker: Something you don't want to see flying out of the bush at you if you are in the jungle.

Twin: Someone whom you don't know which is the evil one until it's too late.

Twit: Anyone who is out for your job.

Two-faced: Anyone who is out for your job.

Typewriter: An ancient device used by primitives that resembles the modern keyboard.

Typical: Most attitudes.

Tyranny: How most multi-billion-dollar companies are overseen.

Udder: Cow titty.

Ugly: A characteristic of human nature.

Ukulele: A baby guitar.

Ulcer: Something that grows bigger every time I hear my ex's voice on the answering machine.

Ulterior: The average motive.

Ultimate: The state of your power depending on how much money you have in the bank.

Umbilical: Usually cut at birth, but some young adults in their twenties still seem to have one attached.

Umbrella: Portable lightning rod.

Umpire: A guy who has 20/20 vision as long as he's not standing on grass.

Unacceptable: The behavior of most teenagers.

Unaccommodating: What any hotel is if you have a coupon.

Unaccountable: Congressional back-door politics.

Unaccustomed: What we have become with regard to genuine courtesy (not that fake courtesy they make you have when you work in a department store).

Unappreciated: A waitress, the clerk at the supermarket, or any fast food restaurant employee.

Unapproachable: Any woman who ranks at least an eight if you are not a ten.

Unarmed: Security guards.

Unattractive: You to anyone ranking above an eight (see Unapproachable).

Unbearable: Modern hip-hop or rap music.

Unchallenged: Political decisions.

Uncivilized: Most people at the dinner table.

Unclean: Most people on the subway.

Uncomfortable: How I feel about the above-mentioned people.

Uncommunicative: My ex about it is anything I might need.

Unconscious: Something I am bored into by most conversations.

Unconstitutional: Seems to pertain to most recent laws, depending upon your political party.

Uncontrollable: Any American four year old.

Uncouth: Your daughter's boyfriend.

Uncover: Something that is very dangerous to do if someone in government did it.

Under: Where most people are in reference to their boss's thumb.

Undercover: Where the best two activities are performed (sleep being one).

Undergraduate: Something that not enough students ever get past.

Underhanded: The way that most people feel as though they have been dealt with by any cellular phone company.

Understand: What people pretend to do when you give directions.

Undervalued: Anything you sell to a pawnbroker.

Underwear: Wedgie handle.

Undesirable: My job.

Undignified: The family of the groom.

Undress: Something you have to tip for in certain clubs.

Uneducated: Most Americans due to federal guidelines.

Unemployed: Most Americans due to federal guidelines.

Unqualified: What most people are for the good jobs.

Uneven: Your fair share.

Unexpected: S.W.A.T. when they break in your door at two in the morning.

Unfair: Employee benefit package.

Unfaithful: Your spouse.

Unfamiliar: Your teenage children.

Unfashionable: Your wardrobe.

Unfathomable: Your credit card debt.

Unfavorable: What you are to your boss.

Unfeeling: Anyone you tell your problems to.

Unfinished: Anything in your garage.

Unfit: Your physical condition.

Unforeseen: Your kid's dental bills.

Unforgiving: The credit agency handling your dental bills.

Unfortunate: The state of your bank account after the above.

Unfounded: The cost of your kid's braces.

Unfriendly: The credit agency trying to collect the debt from the braces.

Unfunded: The cost of your kid's braces.

Unfurnished: Your home after your kid gets braces.

Ungainly: Your kid with ugly braces.

Ungentlemanly: Your attitude after your kid gets braces.

Ungodly: Additional charges after you thought your payment plan for the braces was all set.

Ungrateful: Your kid's attitude about those ridiculously expensive braces.

Unhappy: The true state of human existence.

Unhealthy: Most of what you eat.

Unheard: Anything your wife says while you are watching the game.

Unification: All talk and no action.

Uniform: Scares your dog.

Unimaginable: Your kid's report card with all A's.

Unimpeachable: Modern American presidents.

Unimportant: Any announcement made by your boss.

Unimproved: The condition of the average public school.

Uninhabited: What the school music room will soon be (also the gym and the art room).

Uninstructed: What the students in public school will soon be.

Unintelligible: The grammar and handwriting of those students in public schools.

Unintentional: The actions of the teachers in public schools.

Uninterested: The state of mind of those students in public schools.

Uninteresting: The learning materials in public schools.

Uninviting: Parent night at school.

Union: Part of the problem with public schools.

Unique: Every child, which is why the public school problems shouldn't be allowed to continue.

Universal: The language of the almighty dollar.

Unjust: Divorce court.

Unkind: Divorce attorneys.

Unknown: Anything in a legal document, to the layman.

Unlicensed: How most people drive.

Unlucky: Lottery fanatics.

Unmanageable: Your hair if you own a motorcycle.

Unnoticed: You at the prom.

Unoccupied: Your car's back seat at the prom.

Unopposed: What your prom date was to the quarterback while you were getting her punch.

Unpaid: What you feel after taxes and child support comes out of your check.

Unpalatable: Fast food.

Unpleasant: The breath of the guy next to you on the bus.

Unpopular: You in high school.

Unpublished: Most real literature (this got published, didn't it?).

Unread: Porno magazines.

Unregistered: Grandpa's gun.

Unreliable: Any witness your kid produces when he is in trouble.

Unromantic: Lingerie for *her* birthday?

Unsatisfactory: Any work your husband does on the yard.

Unsavory: The meal you cook when he screws up the yard.

Unsoiled: The best way to find your two year olds underwear.

Unspeakable: The lyrics of most hip-hop or rap music.

Unstable: Any Hollywood relationship.

Unsuccessful: Most blind dates.

Untie: What most people wish they could do with the knot after the wedding.

Untrue: Seemingly, most campaign advertisements.

Untrustworthy: The sources for those campaign advertisements.

Unwarranted: Accusations in those campaign advertisements.

Unwholesome: What they are trying to make the other guy look like in the campaign ad so you won't see how bad they are.

Unworthy: What most people are to their titles.

Uphill: Seems like, every little thing you have to do in life.

Urine: Spring water for pirates.

Useless: Anything you buy with a label that reads, "as seen on TV."

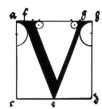

Vacancy: A sign that should be worn across most people's foreheads.

Vacant: What most landlords of section eight housing wish their properties were.

Vacation: Something I very desperately need.

Vaccination: What they call it at the doctor's office when they stick your baby with needles full of nasty stuff that you find out years later either doesn't work or caused something even worse than the disease it supposedly vaccinated against.

Vacuum: The space often found between a set of ears.

Vagina: A lovely thing.

Vague: Any description given by a politician.

Vain: What the truth is often pleaded to the average judge in.

Valentine: Some holiday they made up to guilt us into buying more crap.

Valet: The guy who steals all the change out of your ashtray.

Valiant: A word that has not been used to describe anyone for a long time.

Valid: What your word is not in court.

Valueless: Modern collectibles.

Vampire: Tabloid photographer.

Vandalism: Censorship.

Vanilla: What they call you when you don't want to do anything kinky.

Vanish: Depending on what country you live in, what may happen to you if you vote the wrong way.

Vanity: What famous people have.

Vanquish: What we seem to do to countries that cannot defend themselves.

Vaporize: To cut one in the elevator.

Variable: Any promise made by someone working for government.

Variety: Why I like the buffet.

Vasectomy: A very horrible operation that takes all the fun out of climaxing.

Vassalage: It used to mean "dependent servitude"; now I think it refers to supermarket and department store employees.

Vegetarian: Someone who is mocked by people who eat steroid-laced and disease-ridden meat.

Vegetation: The act of spending most of your time watching prime time television.

Veneration: Withheld from those who deserve it and showered on those who do not.

Vengeance: What too many people seem to be fueled by nowadays.

Ventilation: Something there should be more of in public restrooms.

Ventilator: A device used by a long-time former smoker.

Ventriloquist: What your average billion-dollar corporation is to your average senator.

Verbalism: Something expressed orally (that's what it really means but I like the definition).

Verbosity: Blithering endlessly; any speech in Congress.

Verisimilar: Appearing truthful; any speech in Congress.

Vertebrate: Having a spine; lacking in any speech made in Congress.

Veteran: A person who is ignored by the government after having been terribly taken advantage of in all things (until the government needs them).

Veto: What the president does when he doesn't get his way.

Viagra: An erectile dysfunction drug made from a secret ingredient which is a compound extracted from my workout sweat.

Vibrator: Ask your wife.

Vice: What you feel like you are in when you are part of the menial labor workforce.

Vice President: Who? I can't remember who that is.

Victim: One of a vast number of persons worldwide who will never receive help from his government or law enforcement.

Victimize: What elected officials do to voters after the election.

Villa: What you call your house when you are rich.

Violence: The only thing that some people understand.

Violinist: A dying breed, now that we have synthesizers.

Virgin: Getting harder and harder to find.

Visitation: Certain times of the day in which women line up at the prison with infants and toddlers.

Vocabulary: A lacking ingredient in the average American.

Vodka: How they deal with poverty in Russia.

Vogue: Temporary fashion (think about it).

Voiceless: Any person with no political connections at a town meeting.

Volume: What you crank up in your car so you can slowly go deaf.

Volunteer: Sucker.

Vote: Doesn't count as much as you think.

Voter: Easily duped person; usually elderly.

Voucher: What you get when you are poor instead of help.

Vulture: Any person involved in advertising.

Wad: You could find one stuck in your crack if you weren't careful.

Waddle: How you walk home after the club's bouncer takes your keys.

Wade: What you do in the pool when you are too much of a wimp for the deep end.

Wager: Not always as friendly as you would are led to believe.

Wagon: More people fall off of this than they would ever admit.

Wail: How the baby makes sure you are still up at 2:30 in the morning.

Waist: If you're lucky, it's the lowest of three numbers on your blind date's measurements.

Waiter: A man who lives for tips and verbal abuse.

Waitress: The female version of above but with sexual harassment added in.

Wake: The most depressing meal you will ever have (unless you are burying a real asshole).

Walking: When this was declared to be an exercise, it was proof that we are in a sad state of affairs.

Wallet: Something you should never keep in your back or jacket pocket when riding the subway.

Wallflower: Me at a party.

Wallow: What most people do with misery instead of looking for solutions.

Wane: What your penis did before Viagra.

War: Extremely profitable for business.

Wardrobe: Out of style before you know it and back in twenty years later.

Warfare: Rarely seen up close by those who start it.

Warlike: Always the other guy...

Warp: What tends to be done to the truth by the time it makes it to press.

Warrant: What they use to drag you off for parking meter violations while mass murderers run around unchecked.

Wart: Auntie says it's a birthmark, but we know better.

Washboard: The stomach of every guy but you.

Wasteful: What people indigenous to industrialized countries are.

Watching: What most people are content with instead of doing.

Waterfall: Nature's showers.

Waterproof: Dirty children.

Watertight: What a cheater thought his alibi was, before daytime talk shows started using lie detectors.

Wax: Potato farm found in the ear.

Wealth: A dream for some and a nightmare for others.

Weapon: Words, more often than tools.

Weary: The soul of the pure for the rest of the wicked.

Weather forecaster: Just another man who promises twelve inches and gives you three.

Weather-beaten: Just about every farmhouse I've ever seen.

Weather-wise: The opposite of any meteorologist.

Wedlock: Invisible chains and a deadbolt.

Weed: So much easier to grow than grass, it makes me wonder why we bother with the grass.

Weird: Coming up with the idea to rewrite the dictionary.

Welfare: Probably the most ripped off and exploited of all federally funded programs. Or, the modern version of "bread and circus" (i.e., hush money for the poor).

Wench: The girl at the end of the bar they keep warning you about.

Werewolf: Me after five days without a razor.

Western: A movie theme that they just don't seem to be able to get right anymore.

Wet nurse: A woman who would get paid a lot better if she serviced adults.

Whalebone: Not worth the fines.

Whatever: A response that means "please smack me in the mouth," (when spoken by a teenager).

Wheeze: How a smoker breathes.

Whine: A tone that means "please smack me in the mouth," (when used by an elementary-school-aged child).

Whipping: Often threatened by parents (seldom carried out).

Whisky: Dad hides a bottle of this in the bookshelf, in the closet, in the spare tire, under the mattress, in the tank behind the toilet, under the refrigerator, etc., etc., etc.

Whiz: How you write in the snow (harder for girls).

Wicked: Most decisions involving healthcare.

Wife: The woman who runs you into bankruptcy and makes you lose all of your friends, then leaves you and gets you for alimony and child support after she moves you out of *your* house.

Wig: Easier to spot than you think, "*baldy*".

Wimp: The average parent when it comes to disciplining his child.

Wind: Deadly when broken in an enclosed space.

Wind bag: Any city's mayor at a charity function.

Wine: Grown-up grape juice.

Wine taster: A pretty cushy job if you ask me.

Wing commander: Really cool-sounding job title.

Winner: Not always as big of a deal as it's made out to be.

Wireless: How you trade mobility for static.

Wisdom tooth: Must not be very wise, since it's almost always pulled.

Wish: What we do instead of succeed.

Witchcraft: Not as scary in real life.

Withdrawal: Easier at the ATM than with the teller.

Without: What most people make do with.

Withstand: What we are forced to do when dealing with the bad manners and tempers of others.

Witness: The person you intimidate out of a trial.

Womanish: Most guys on the boulevard.

Woodpecker: Prosthetic penis.

Work: Slave labor.

Working-class: Miserable peons.

Working day: Too damn long.

Workmanship: Quality you don't see any more.

World-wide: Where your personal business ends up when you're a celebrity.

Worm: The celebrity's agent.

Worship: The celebrity's fan club's pastime.

Worst: The above-mentioned people when you see them up close.

Wrathful: Your wife if you come home smelling of perfume.

Wreckage: Your car when if your wife gets her hands on it after your pitiful explanation for the above.

Wrestler: An athletic person in underwear, who is a poor actor, yet wears the brand of a hero or villain, thanks to the media.

Wrinkle: Easily removed with long, painful surgery.

X-rays: How they permeate you with radiation in the hospital.

Xenophobe: Depending on what part of the country you live in, a person who fears either extraterrestrials, or other types of aliens (currently Mexicans).

Xylophagous: Really, *really* hungry (hey, it's the letter X, I'm trying).

Xylophone: A baby's toy, no matter how good you are at it.

Xyster: One of those things the surgeon doesn't let you see before the operation.

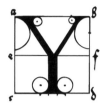

Yacht: Luxury rowboat.

Yachting: A made-up sport for the ridiculously wealthy.

Yachtsman: A man in a sweater and a captain's hat who is not a captain, and who sips a martini while other people race so he can get the trophy (see above).

Yahoo: Hillbilly battle cry.

Yak: A smelly, furry cow.

Yankee: They once got a great trade and left behind the curse of the bambino (you have to be from Boston to get that one).

Yap: What we do too much of when we should be minding our own business.

Year: Shorter than it seems, even as it seems to take forever.

Yearbook: Another way for the school to gouge your wallet.

Yeast: The penalty for avoiding abstinence.

Yeehaw: Redneck battle cry.

Yellow: Your average security guard.

Yeoman: A really gay way to say "farmer."

Yes: What she really means when she says it.

Yesterday: When you should have done what you are now finally catching up on.

Youth: One of our most wasted resources.

Zareba: Zebra for people who can't spell.

Zebra: The right way to spell it.

Zeppelin: The greatest rock band who ever lived.

Zigzag: The true angles being run when a person tells you that they are on the straight and narrow path.

Zircon: What your engagement ring is made of.

Zodiac: Something too many people rely upon when they are too wishy-washy to make their own decisions in life.

Zone: What you're in when you hit ninety miles an hour on the freeway.

Zoo: Where we keep all the animals on display to save them from ourselves.